GOD,

I DON'T NEED

A MIRACLE

TOMORROW...

I NEED ONE TODAY

One Man's Journey Of Faith Against All Odds

By

Mark Burchell

AUTHOR'S ACKNOWLEDGEMENTS

This book is dedicated to the four generations of my family that are alive and serving God in Champions Church today.

The twenty-year journey up to now has been long and hard; it has been rewarding beyond description. Thankfully, I have not travelled the journey alone, as for most of the time, I have had the privilege of sharing it with my greatest and most loyal supporters.

Firstly, my mom and dad who have lived through all of the changes and survived to tell the tale.

My wife Gillian, who beyond a shadow of a doubt has not only helped me become the person I am today, but has shaped the way that Champions is today.

My three children, Esther (Adam – my son-in-law), Joshua and Caleb who have seen the tears and been part of the heartaches as well as the joys, and have made me very proud to be their dad, and of course the fourth generation, namely our new grandson, Noah Freedom, who will only ever know the new spiritual home and will never be embarrassed to say to his mates, "That's my Church."

Thank you, also, to the rest of my family along with the wonderful staff, pastors, leaders and congregation of Champions Church, without whom the Dream would never have become a reality – I love you.

Finally my thanks must always go to Jesus Christ, who not only saved me and changed my life, but who also called me to make sure I leave behind more than what I started with.

It is my greatest desire that as you laugh and cry your way through this book that you too will be inspired to know a miracle-working God for yourself and that with Him, nothing is impossible.

Enjoy x.

CONTENTS

CHAPTER 1

The Start of Things to Come – Age Five

All the days ordained for me were written in your book before one of them came to be.

Psalm 139 v 16

Miss Ellington's voice was quiet but firm.

'Write down your date of birth at the top of your paper,' she said.

It was my first day at Sledmere Primary School, and after the first half an hour, I was beginning to hate it. I sat there, embarrassed. I knew I was born on a Wednesday, but, at the age of five, I'd never really memorised my date of birth or, to be more precise, the exact year. All the other kids seemed to know theirs and somehow this didn't seem the time to start to start copying; that came later. Thankfully, my teacher found my details from my registration form and I breathed a big sigh of relief. I now knew I when I was born.

The event happened on 7th of June 1961, in Dudley, West Midlands, the middle child of Denis and Gwen Burchell. Had I been born a girl, I was to be called Yvonne. Thankfully (no offence to any Yvonnes out there), I came out a boy, and the one thing I had remembered was my name – Mark.

I soon discovered that compared to many of the other kids in the class, I was extremely shy, easily embarrassed, and not as intelligent as they were. I hate the thought of being shown up for getting answers wrong, and the fear of being asked to say something in front of the whole class gripped me with terror if I sensed that was about to happen.

'Why do you keep covering your work, Mark Burchell?' said Mr Woodhall, the maths teacher, as he peered over my shoulder. I just looked up with sad and embarrassed eyes and carried on. The real reason was that deep down, I lacked confidence, and secretly feared being made an example for getting my work wrong. Also, I blushed very easily and that, along with my shy disposition, meant I was a prime candidate to be picked on by all and sundry.

For some reason, Mr Woodhall took a shine to me, possibly because he saw that I was struggling. Over time, one of the things that really impressed and inspired me about him was that he was a talented musician.

He encouraged me to join his guitar class, which I absolutely loved and thrived on, but most of all, he took the time and trouble on the odd occasion to bring to school, his all-singing-all-dancing Wurlitzer organ, which he played in front of all the kids some wintery lunchtimes in the school hall, an event that became the highlight in the school term.

Wow, I wish I could do that, I thought, not realising the power of those few words was soon about to come true. I was desperate to play the piano, the organ, or any musical instrument. Whenever I could, I

2

did anything that allowed me to tinkle the old ivories of the school grand piano on the stage. So much so, that my mom and dad were convinced that I had a hidden talent, and they decided to take up the offer of a free, old honky-tonk piano, from an old lady that they knew.

When it arrived, it was really just one big eyesore as a piece of furniture in the front room, but it did the job for a time. I started to have piano lessons, and enjoyed the fact that at least now, I could do something that most of the kids at school couldn't. Very quickly, I found that I could memorise pieces of music and even play the piano by ear.

Sitting cross-legged in assembly one morning, and listening to yet another monotone ditty from Mr Burrows, the headmaster, I noticed that Miss Richards, our gorgeous music teacher, was missing from behind the grand piano high up on the stage that morning.

'We will now sing hymn number 301,' Mr Burrows bellowed out.

Great! This meant the assembly was coming to a close. After a short pause and some whisperings at the front with Mr Bradford, the 6'7" maths teacher, I heard my name being called.

'Is Mark Burchell here today?'

My heart began to race as I responded with a nervous quiver. 'Yes, sir.'

'Then come and play the hymn for us, Amazing Grace.'

I was now just eight years old. I slowly got to my feet, and walked out of my line, aware that all four hundred and something eyes were now on me. It seemed to take forever to walk up those stage steps to the seat of the grand piano with its top open wide.

Thankfully, the one thing I could do was play from memory, and I had learnt 'Amazing Grace' because it was so easy to play, complete with an added extra – a key change on the last verse!

When it was all over I was relieved, but actually I found that I had enjoyed it, so much so that I went on to learn and memorise every hymn that we sang, and, whenever Miss Richards was away, I played in front of the whole school.

Mr Bradford, the tall one, had always mourned the fact that he had never learnt to play the piano, so twice a week, he asked me to teach him during lunch breaks. I was just a boy, and for me to try and get his long, gangly fingers on the right notes was not easy. Apart from a one-fingered tune, 'O have you seen my elephant?' he never did progress any further.

Looking back, I now think that God had planned my first public appearance just so that I would never forget the theme for the rest of my life:

Amazing Grace
How sweet the sound
That saved a wretch like me
I once was lost but now I'm found
Was blind but now I see.

CHAPTER 2

Surviving the Sunday Services

Train a child in the way he should go, and when he is old he will not depart from it.

Proverbs 22 v 6

Sundays in our home were always a three-lap endurance test, with the family going to the Baptist Chapel in the nearby town of Netherton. Three times, every Sunday, we walked the two-mile round trip to Sweet Turf, as it was called, which I later found out originated from its 1810 roots, when Netherton was farmland. The cows had long since gone from the sweet pasture land that the Church now stood on, along with any signs that of life that one time it may have shown years earlier. I always did find it a bit of an embarrassment when I was asked what Church I went to; the answer 'Sweet Turf' didn't quite often give off the impression of the hippest place in town.

The Church consisted of fifteen people, most of them elderly family members, or people connected to the family in some way. My older brother John and myself used to entertain ourselves during the services, which always seemed to last for hours (an hour and a quarter to be precise), by eating a selection of sweets and Dolly mixtures that were distributed quietly to us at the start of each sermon by Nan Burchell, who was designated as our minder on the morning shift. We would place the sweets between the hymn book and its hard cover, sit on the book at the start of the sermon and, one by one, ease them out so that no one detected the process taking place during what my nan described later as a 'very deep sermon'; being translated, 'I didn't understand a word, but I'm too polite to admit it!' Anyway, once the nearly flattened sweets had all gone and the sermon hadn't, it was now time to sketch the various people from behind, all of which had nicknames. Noddy Frog was my favourite.

Uncle Horace had been playing the pipe organ for the last fifty years, but somehow, even to my young musical ear, had obviously not improved with time. His forte was the anthems he played during the collection. The only problem was that it only took about sixty seconds to collect money from fifteen people, if that, but his shortened anthem was around the four-minute mark, so the shortfall in the collection time was made up every Sunday by Uncle Horace's funeral music, as we called it.

Once again, the years of experience had not taught him to stop halfway through, so he just carried on until the music ran out. For this, another family member despised him and used tuts, coughs, sighs and the occasional slamming of the glasses case on the front pew to signify 'stop or else', but he never did.

Light relief came upon the Church when I was

appointed as the deputy Church organist at fifteen. One of the finest pipe organists around taught me at 9 o'clock every Sunday morning for three years, so that by the time I was seventeen, the sixteen local Churches all around our town wanted to hire me (for nothing of course) for their yearly Sunday school anniversary services. This was quite flattering, as I got to play on a whole variety of organs, including the one at Messiah Baptist Church. History has it that it housed Cromwell and his troops at the invasion of Dudley Castle in the 1600s. On that particular Sunday, the Church of course was packed and I played full throttle for some of the great old hymns. The funny thing was, the very next day the building surveyors arrived to take a look at the dry rot and there and then rendered the building unsafe and stated that under no circumstance must the Church organ be played, as it could bring the place down. Oh well, we survived another Sunday.

Rolling out of bed one Sunday morning, I made my way to the early morning Easter Communion service. On this particular Sunday, it was held at our Church, but was a combined service for the Churches in the town. Bleary eyed by the early hour, I found myself strangely emotional as I played for the third hymn. The congregation sang with great gust, the chorus...

Mine, mine, mine

Dear Saviour thou art mine,

I know thou art mine.

Those old words seemed to penetrate my young heart and tears streamed down my face as I played like never before. I think that was the day I became a born-again Christian; if not, then I knew at least I was on the road to becoming a proper Christian, and Jesus became real to me that day.

Not long after that experience, I found myself nervously standing in the little school room at the back of the old chapel, and there I read out my testimony, as to what had happened to me, something that had to be done in front of Church members who judged whether or not you were genuine in following the Lord. A good outcome from this meeting meant you were put forward for Baptism at the next available slot; a slot that no one had filled for a good few years. Little did I know what this really entailed, but I was soon to find out…!

I had seen some black, dusty, damp-smelling robes hanging in one of the back classrooms of the Sunday school for years, but had assumed that they belonged to the choir that had thankfully, so I presumed, died off years earlier. I assumed about the robes that is, wrongly.

The robes turned out to be the compulsory dress code for all candidates for Baptism, which was a grand total of one – me. Baptisms were few and far between, so when I walked out from the back room into the Church that night, I nearly died. Not only was the downstairs of the Church full, but the whole balcony as well, and into the bargain, as I looked up, I began to spot school friends, even teachers, who had come to gawp at me getting wet.

I had never seen so many people in our little Church, and they had never seen me dressed like Batman either! Yet once again, I survived another Sunday, and I am sure that I stood up as a witness for Jesus, even though I did feel like a wally.

Around that time, Uncle Stanley, one of the Church leaders, began to fulfil a lifelong ambition at seventy-three. He had always wanted to be part of a brass band, or at least conduct one. Why he had a degree in playing the violin I forgot to ask, but somehow, he managed to secure some local funding and purchased enough instruments to start the 'Sweet Turf Brass Band'. Thursday nights were designated as 'Band Practice', and although he had never played a wind instrument in his life, he became an overnight expert in anything from the cornet to the tuba.

The band mainly consisted of family members plus a few others. Amazingly, after a lot of hard work, laughing, fooling around, and fetching Uncle Stanley back after he'd walked out yet again because of our frivolity, we succeeded in becoming a well-known brass band with more bookings than we could handle.

I will never forget the one cold December night, when we were due to play at 'The Hen and Chickens' social club in Wolverhampton. We were positioned on stage behind closed curtains, waiting to be announced to a packed audience as the Support Act to a local well-known celebrity group, 'Giggity'. Instruments were held in place, lips nervously poised ready to blow a triumphant first note, the announcer cued the curtains, and as we faced the waiting crowd, not a sound came out. I was now peering from behind my B-flat bass on the back row, and all I could hear was loud whispers from the front brass section. 'Stan! Stan!' Uncle Stanley was perched on the front row of the audience, baton at the ready, but fast asleep! I can only think that the folks at the club thought it was part of the act, as they loved it, and went back several times over the years.

CHAPTER 3

One Amazing Encounter

**'For I know the plans I have for you,' declares the
Lord. 'Plans to prosper you and not harm you. Plans
to give you a hope and a future.'**
Jeremiah 29 v 11

By the summer of 1978, I had bought a 50cc
motorbike, and was enjoying the freedom of being
able to get around under my own steam. This made
a nice change to the previous years of walking and
going everywhere on push-bike. Sundays came
around so fast, particularly as I was now working
part-time after school at the local butcher's shop
three nights a week, plus Saturday mornings. This was
in addition to working as a cashier at the local petrol
station until 10 p.m. two or three nights a week, for
50p an hour. Little did I know that this Sunday would
be yet another of those different days that would
affect the rest of my life for the better.

Every Church in Netherton had an annual Sunday
School Anniversary that began with what was called
'a procession of witness'. Today, it was the turn of
Cole Street Methodist Church, who had invited the
Sweet Turf Brass Band to lead their particular

procession. It was a beautiful day, and as we trudged around various streets with me carrying an enormous B-flat bass, I was aware that some of the teenage girls from Cole Street Church were nervously giggling as some of the youngest band members and I were draining spit out of our instrument at the end of every hymn. On this particular day, I was wearing my new leather motorcycle jacket that had three red stripes down the left-hand side, and whether it was this, or the sight of my inviting red lips tingling from the third time playing 'Summer Suns Are Glowing' that attracted one young lady, I do not know. What I do know was that a certain Gillian Felton had picked me out and said, 'He's nice.'

I've never believed in luck, chance, or fate; but I have always believed in destiny. 'Coincidence,' said someone, 'is simply a God co-ordinated incident,' and today was one of those. That evening, I rushed out of the evening service at my own Church, got onto my motorbike, and sped off to the petrol station where my best mate, Andy Watchorn, was on duty as cashier until ten o'clock that night. As we chatted away, my eyes were drawn to a beautiful young girl who was walking past the garage along with her mate. Unfortunately for me, there was a boyfriend in tow and my heart sank as I thought about the fact that she was already spoken for. I was still fairly shy at seventeen, and Andy knew that it didn't take much to make me blush. Less than half an hour later, my heart leapt, as the very same came back up the road with her friend, this time minus the boyfriend. YES! Without me saying a word, Andy was frantically knocking the window to attract their attention, whilst at the same time, he was trying to signal to the two bewildered girls that I was hiding underneath the counter.

'You idiot,' I said, 'you've frightened them off,' as we watched them scurry up the road giggling. However, just before closing time, they reappeared and perched themselves on the wall at the entrance to the garage. *This is a sure sign that they must like us,* I thought to myself. There was no escaping now. There was only one way out, and as soon as Andy had cashed up, I put on my full-face helmet, went outside and got on my motorbike. Even though I was shy, I couldn't help but ride over to the two girls and turn the engine off, especially as it felt fairly safe because they could not really see me blushing beneath the helmet. She was even more beautiful up close, and before I could say anything, her friend blurted out, 'She fancies you! She saw you in the band this morning and she recognises your jacket.' I was stunned, elated, scared, and I can't remember what else. All I knew is that we were made for each other. Gillian, as it turned out only lived a few doors up from the petrol station, so from then on she would pop down to see me whenever I was on duty. To cut out all the minor details, she duly dumped her current boyfriend in preference for me! Little did I know that at that moment, we had just both seemingly bumped into destiny and would be married six years later. I still look back 30 years on and think, HOW AWESOME is the plan of God for our lives, that on the very same day in history, we would meet each other twice, on the very same day and fall in love.

CHAPTER 4

Surprised by God

In his heart a man plans his course, but the Lord determines his steps.

Proverbs 16 v 9

On leaving secondary school, I found myself at the Catering College in Halesowen, three miles away, where I was about to embark on the pathway to my choice of career: to became a professional French chef. From junior school age, I had shown a keen interest in cookery. Every Saturday morning, I would insist on making the family apple pies, while the other kids were playing outside or watching TV. This developed into a bit of a specialty of mine, and when the time came, I chose the cookery course option in my secondary school. The cookery class at Hillcrest School turned out to be a joke, as the word 'cooker' seemed to be interpreted as 'doss around' by all the other kids, mainly the worst ones in our school. 'Fanny Hill' as we called Miss Hill, the cookery teacher, after the famous television cook 'Fanny Craddock', lost control of us from day one. Frequently, the Head would appear after yet another uncontrollable quiche-making session, when she would storm out shouting her famous last words: 'Cut the Cackle!'

The day came when the most picked on, and not so intelligent pupil, nicknamed 'Cocoa Beana' (mainly because he had hair like the bristles of a coconut), caught a missive glob of pastry flying through the air in his left eye. Everybody thought that it had blinded him, but fortunately, after a short moment, he came around with sight back to normal and a red eye. I think it was from that moment that Miss Hill took a turn for the worse, and turned up less frequently to our class. It was sometime later that we learned that she had had a mental breakdown. To this day, I fear I know how it happened: Class C3.

The final year of my schooling quickly approached, with preparation for the exams becoming more and more of a daily burden; particularly to people like myself, who had only got to go to Hillcrest School by failing the last lot of official exams when I was eleven, known as the '11+'. I can remember well, the summer of that final year being particularly hot and suffering from hay fever.

Not being one to miss out on an opportunity for sunbathing, I decided, one Thursday afternoon, to revise for the Chemistry exam, whilst lying in the garden in just my bathers. Unfortunately, I hadn't read the timetable correctly, and had no idea that at the precise moment that I was now dozing in the lounger, the Deputy Head was frantically ringing the doorbell and explaining to my shocked mother that her son was now late for his Chemistry exam by twenty minutes. By the time I got dressed and raced to the school on my moped, the exam was already in full swing. It was hardly surprising then, that I obtained the lowest possible mark, which considering I only turned up halfway through, I didn't think was too bad a result.

Little did I know that was not the end of my days' altercation with the senior staff of the school. The moment I walked out of the exam, I was accosted by the Head himself who wanted to know why a pupil parked his motorbike, illegally, in the staff car park!

When the exam results came through, the biggest surprise was achieving an O level pass in English Literature. The biggest shock was for my parents, who had raised me in Church and Sunday School, only to find that I'd got another lowest possible grade, this time in Religious Education. Oh well, it only goes to prove that if at first you don't succeed... you're quite normal!

So here I was, I'd just scraped through to get a place at Halesowen Catering College, which helped me focus enormously on the gift I was now beginning to realise, lay within me.

Chosen to represent the college in my second year, with a group of five other 'elite' students, we found ourselves travelling to a top hotel in London. We were finalists in the 'taste of England' competition, and impressed the top panel of judges with our menu planning and culinary skills so much that we carried off the first prize in the whole of the country. I still have the silver salver today, even though I've considered selling it several times in the not-so-well-off times in our lives.

Myself and Gillian were still an item during this time, so much so that I carried the words 'Mark loves Gill' on the top box of my motorbike for everyone to see. I was proud of her, even though we were to fall out several times before we fell back for good.

In the summer of 1979, I completed my catering degree, and for the first time in my life, I left college with credit passes in every object. This meant I was now a fully qualified chef, waiter, wine-waiter. But also for the first time in my life, I was now feeling pressure to succeed like never before.

I had become good friends with some really great chefs, one in particular who was to go on to the Savoy Hotel in London, and then to become the England Football team chef, and still is today, as well as owning two successful restaurants in the area. London was definitely the place to go, and so I gave in to the pressure and decided to turn my back on my home life, Church life and my girlfriend. Gillian said to me during the decision-making process, 'It's either me or London.' I decided to go to London. She promptly dumped me.

I got an interview for a job in a small French restaurant in Harrow, London, just outside Wembley. I decided, after being asked to take the job, that I really would go, and so off I set with my belongings. Deep down, I knew that I was breaking my parents' hearts, especially as I commuted back and forth on my upgraded 200cc motorbike.

By the start of the second month, I was promoted from 'commis' (skivvy) to Second Chef. This basically meant I ran the place when the Head Chef was not around. Despite my apparent quick success, the high-life of London was for me nothing but the low life. I hated it. I missed home, my girlfriend (ex) and knew that I was a runaway from God and could not escape. Even the Head Chef's sister and brother-in-law walked through the kitchen holding a Bible – I couldn't get away from His presence.

I decided that I need to look for work a little closer to home, and amazingly, I landed a job interview at a beautiful thirty-seater French restaurant, above a nice pub in a small area called the Clent, near to Hagley, West Midlands. I got the job because my college tutor recommended me. Without any hesitation, I handed in my notice in London, much to the dismay of my former employers. I had lasted only six weeks away from home!

On the very day that I arrived back, there was excitement in Netherton. Don't get me wrong, It wasn't over my return, but over the stories that many people, particularly the young ones, were becoming born-again Christians at the tent crusade held on my old school playing fields. Two of the people who were 'saved' were Stephanie, my younger sister, and Gillian, my ex-girlfriend. Both apparently had gone forward at the end of the message to receive Jesus Christ. This intrigued me, as well as made me somewhat envious that I had missed it all, whatever 'it all' was.

Fortunately for me, there was just one night left, and I was determined not to miss it. I sat with my brother John on the fourth row back, and when the evangelist got up to speak, it was just as if he were speaking to me from the beginning to end. I was under deep conviction about the state of my life, and found myself uncontrollably sobbing, much to my embarrassment. That night, I knew God had re-captured my heart, and that I would never look back again. I recommitted my life to Jesus Christ.

The day after, I went to find Gillian, and asked her about what had happened to her life. I desperately wanted it to be real for her, as I now knew that we should be back together, but both as committed Christians this time. I found her working in the local post office, and after giving her the signal to pop outside, we exchanged some quick niceties, confirmed that she had become a Christian, and promptly got back together again.

It was to be nearly two years later that we found ourselves under canvas again, at the big top Spring Harvest, a national Christian festival held at Butlins Holiday Camp, in Prestatyn of all places. The weather was cold and wet that Easter time, but with 5,000 other bodies inside, we didn't particularly notice. Plus the fact we had our love to keep us warm, this time forever.

The freedom of the big top meetings was wonderful, with amazing worship that was so new to both of us, having been brought up in traditional Churches on a diet of hymn and prayer sandwiches. Little did I know that week, that the whole future of my life would change forever as I was about to be surprised by God.

It was halfway through the week and David Pawson was now well into his message based around a fairly obscure text from the Bible, 'A little Child Shall Lead Them'. He spoke of the need for new leaders to emerge for the 21st century; once again God was about to zap me inside a tent. I knew that God was calling me, and at the end of the message, I quickly responded with around 200 other folk that night. As I walked forward, my eyes streamed with tears, and now it was as if it was just me and God. I remember being ushered into a counselling room, which was one of Butlins old theatres. 'Please take your seats, and someone will come and talk to you in a moment,' one of the officials said.

I remember thinking, *I don't need anybody to counsel me, God is doing it right now, all on His own.*

I sat there, cocooned in His presence. He was so real, that through my sobbing, I felt like I could ask

Him questions like: 'What's going on here, God?' All of a sudden, I was taken up into a full-colour vision of the dingy back room of the Baptist Chapel back at home. I instantly saw the five faithful pray-ers, that met every Monday night to pray that God would move. Then, all of a sudden, God did a voice over, and the words 'a little child shall lead them' were being spoken over the vision that I saw.

Once again, I asked what this meant, and just as if God was sitting there right next to me, He said so clearly, 'One day you will be the Pastor of that Church.'

I was shocked, elated, mesmerised, and all I could think was, *I have just had an encounter with Almighty God.* Whatever plans I had for my life had just been blown away by that encounter. It would be nearly eight years before I ever told anyone what had happened that night.

CHAPTER 5

Oh, do I like to be beside the seaside

Jesus said, 'Don't be afraid, just believe.'
John 5 v 36

Sometime after my encounter with God, stating that one day I would Pastor the little old Baptist Church, I felt an increasing burden and call to go to Bible College, in order to train for my 'unknown' future. Not being the 'studenty' type, I tried to push it away. After all, I had already done a further two years at Catering College after school, and the thought of a further two didn't really do it for me. It was only when two separate individuals, in the same month, walked up to me and told me that they thought I should train for the future, that my mind was made up.

The big question was, *Where? Where are there any Bible Colleges? How much does it cost? Am I qualified enough to get there?* I decided to flick through any Christian magazines that I could find, hunting for any signs of training places for Chefs who wanted to became Pastors. After months of searching, I narrowed it down to three and decided that because Moorlands Bible College in Bournemouth had the most practical and down to earth course, I would apply to go there and see what happened.

I was filled with excitement and fear at the same time. Going away from home, leaving my girlfriend for weeks at a time, deserting the sinking ship called the Baptist Chapel, and, not least of all, facing the question of 'How will I ever afford it?' certainly filled me with apprehension. Pushing back my fears, I filled in my application form and promptly sent it off, accompanied by a quick prayer that went something like, 'Lord Jesus, don't let me get in if You don't want me to go.' I was about to embark on a brand new journey, and was totally unsure if I should make it or could make it.

Two months later, I was waving goodbye to my parents, as I set off in my Austin Allegro to Christchurch, Bournemouth, on the south coast, for my interview. Scared to death that I wasn't Holy enough to go through the college doors, I soon found the place quite normal with fewer weirdos and super-spirituals than I'd imagined.

After the interviews, where I'd outlined that God had told me my future, I was told that actually I was too young and needed to go back to work for another twelve months, and then I would be accepted. I breathed a sigh of relief as I sped off down Dorset country lanes on my way home, contemplating that I was now going to escape this Bible College thing altogether. Getting married and settling down into my chosen career was now right before me – I'd escaped!

My girlfriend was happy, my mom and dad were happy, my Church was happy, in fact everyone was happy that I wasn't leaving – apart from me. I just knew that this was it. I had to go back in twelve months and secure a place; a place that would prepare me for what lay ahead. I made it clear to everyone that I would be leaving in the next twelve months for the two-year course, and come what may, I had to go. I was being pushed by an invisible force.

As the next twelve months sped up, I began to look at the reality of the fees. I'd calculated that I would need around £3,500 over the next two years; a sum of money in 1982 that might as well have been £35,000. I wondered how on earth I would be able to pay my way.

Once again, faith turned to fear, as I pondered the prospect of not having enough money to fulfil the dream. The turning point came, when I was recommended by a friend to call a certain young man who had recently graduated, and was home from Bible College in England. I dialled his number, and simply asked him what to do, without the money to go. He simply replied, 'Trust God. If it's His will, it's His bill.'

I thanked him politely, but thought, *That's OK for you to say that, but this is me.* I'd never trusted God for money before, and I didn't know how to.

The next morning, it was as if a light had been switched on. *Trusting God,* I thought, *is as simple as it sounds – TRUST GOD – that's it, I'm going to trust God, as he did.*

As September 1982 came closer, I withdrew all of my life-savings out of the Dudley Building Society in order to secure my first couple of terms, plus books etc., a total of £1,500. It felt like the easiest thing in the world to do. My adventure of trusting God had now begun. Little did I know that it would lead in later life to trusting Him for millions.

Nervously, I pulled up to the car park of Moorlands Bible College, already sensing that home sickness was lurking right behind me. Afraid to think about this gigantic step as a home-boy, I threw myself into College life.

I will never forget registration on that first day, as I was told that my first twelve months would be spent sharing with a young man by the name of Keith Kreelman, who, because was traveling by ferry from Ireland, wouldn't be arriving until the next day. Having spent that first night in the room on my own, arranging photographs of family and girlfriend, I was anxious to find out who this Irish guy was. I privately hoped he was a good, plain, old-fashioned Baptist like me. When the door eventually burst open, Keith introduced himself, and quickly told me that he was an Irish, tongue-speaking Pentecostal. Ouch! This was not a good start; a Baptist and a Pentecostal sharing a room that resembled a prison cell. This to me made as much sense as putting a Jack Russell and a Doberman in a cage. Our only saving grace was that we were both madly in love with our girlfriends, whom we planned to marry in two years' time. So we consoled each other as we took it in turns to be homesick for the first week or so. Fearing his Pentecostal beliefs, I chose the top bunk where I thought I would be safely out of the way should he burst into 'Gifts of the Spirit'; something that was foreign and quite wrong for me, I felt. The top bunk was a good choice – that was, until the aroma of Keith's socks in the heat of the day rose to ceiling level and worked its way down to rest on me. What I thought was a temporary sweaty problem in the first few days of not finding the showers, actually turned out to be one of an ongoing source of fun for everyone but me. The only way we could keep things at an acceptable level was to hang his socks out of the window each night ready for the morning. The problem never did get solved – mind you, neither did I ever get a cold.

The sock problem faded into the background as it became painfully aware to him that I didn't share his beliefs, through my indoctrination at the Baptist Chapel. He told me, in no uncertain terms, that I should know and experience the power of God and should speak in tongues. I was offended; or was I intrigued?

Slowly, over the weeks, I let my guard down and began to see the need for the Holy Spirit to touch my life also. Night after night, as I got into my top bunk, long before Keith came into the room, I asked Jesus to give me the gifts of the Holy Spirit so that I could speak in tongues.

Weeks turned to months, as I did everything from opening my mouth wide for a few minutes, to wagging my tongue to see what would happen. I gave up, that was it. *I'm done with it,* I thought. After what seemed like forever, one night, I suddenly started to speak in an unknown, yet incredibly natural language.

'I've got it!' I shouted. 'I've received the Holy Spirit.' I'm not sure who was more pleased – God, Keith or me.

One slight problem remained. However was I going to go back to the Baptist Chapel and not let them know that I'd been filled with the Holy Spirit? Well, God had it worked out perfectly. He was about to do something supernatural that would blow everyone away – including me.

CHAPTER 6

The Power of God

...and the prayer offered in faith will make the sick person well. The Lord will raise him up.

James 5 v 15

The Easter break quickly came around, which gave me an incredible longing for home. I had to wait for six weeks at a time before seeing my family and not least of all my girlfriend; the pain of not being with her was sometimes unbearable. The Easter holidays were second only to the summer in length, so it gave me the opportunity to relax and catch up with as many people as possible. Spring Harvest, the national Christian Convention held in Prestatyn, Wales, was booked by several people from my home town area for that year, which included Gillian and me. As excited to go as we were, there was a problem that lurked in the back of all our minds.

A young man, one of only three from our Church, was seriously ill in bed and due to go to Spring Harvest on the Monday morning. Apparently, his loss of appetite and substantial weight loss while I had been away, had put him in hospital for some time. Although all the tests were inconclusive, nevertheless, his condition was worsening to the degree that each day he would spend 13.5 hours in bed, with the remaining half hour sitting up in bed and attempting to eat a morsel of food. His weight loss and general deterioration was now concerning everybody, particularly his mother who had remained steadfast in her desire to get him to Spring Harvest come what may.

As Easter Monday came for us to travel, he was so ill that his mom decided to create a bed in the back of her estate car by folding the seats down and laying him down as comfortable as possible. The journey turned out to be horrendous, with Mark having to return immediately to his bed-ridden state once he arrived. This time in the cold and damp surroundings of the Butlins Holiday Camp Chalet, which was the accommodation for 5,000 people during that week.

The evening celebrations in the big top tent were incredibly uplifting. It was a far cry from my experiences in the little Baptist Chapel back home. Worship and preaching like I'd never heard it before, moved me to tears most nights, as God's overwhelming presence swept in. The only thing that spoilt it for me, was a still small voice within me that kept telling me to go pray for fourteen-year-old Mark who by all accounts seemed to be dying.

I can't do that, I said back to the voice within, not telling anyone of the inner private battle going on, forgetting that I'd recently asked God to use me with His power. For three whole days and nights, I managed to escape the voice without doing what I was told. The only problem was that with the passing of each hour, came the stronger conviction that I must obey or else. So strong was the feeling, that by the Wednesday night, straight after the big top meeting, I gave up my struggle and shouted out, 'OK, I'll do it!'

I don't think anybody heard me, but instant relief came over me as I obeyed. But now a different problem washed all over me – one of nerves. *What do I do? What shall I say? I've never ever done this before!* However, before I could back out of it again, I darted over to the second-floor chalet and gently knocked on the door and barged in. It was now 9:30 p.m.

A group of friends stood around Mark's bedside, idly chatting and trying to cheer him up as he lay there, skin and bone.

As they turned their attention towards me, I just blurted out, 'I've come to pray for you.' Everybody just smiled at me, and gave me a look of, 'good luck to you then' (Christian good luck, that is). A 'carry on if you dare', kind of thing. I prayed the most weak, simple, yet faith-filled prayer that I had ever prayed and thought to myself, *If that works, I will be amazed,* and then said, 'Amen.'

As I quickly retreated to the door, faith, supernatural faith came all over me, so much so that when Mark's mom met me on the landing, I told her that I had prayed for him, to which she just replied, 'So many people have prayed for him.'

I boldly replied, 'Yes, but this time he'll be alright.'

The conviction in me that night, at twenty-one years of age was unbelievable. I just knew that this young man would be healed, so much so that I could hardly sleep. Early the next morning, I lay in my sleeping bag, thinking, *He's going to be healed.* An hour or so later, word began to spread throughout our group, situated in several different chalets, that the young guy that arrived in the back of a car almost dying, had got out of bed that early morning and cooked breakfast for everyone. It was a miracle. I had never seen such a transformation. Mark was well and truly healed, whole and totally back on his feet, doing everything he could do before. *WOW. What if I hadn't obeyed God?* I thought.

On that day, I realised that my encounter with the Spirit of God on my bunk bed at Bible College was real. By the time we all reached home on the Sunday afternoon, word had already quickly spread about Mark's healing. This was not only new to me, but it was certainly new to the little dwindling congregation at the Sweet Turf Chapel. In fact, it was not only new, it was revolutionary in the impact it had on the 150 years of silence regarding the Holy Spirit and His power.

The very next day after arriving home, I was asked to share at the weekly Monday night prayer meeting, which was usually attended by five people. On this night, it was different; numbers had swelled to almost double. I stood behind the homemade wooden pulpit and spoke nervously about the occurrences of the last few days leading to the miracle. Some were stunned, some were silent, some looked blank, but Mark was living proof of the power of God, as he was there for all to see. No-one could deny that there was a miracle standing before their very eyes.

One thing was for sure, this backstreet, dying Chapel, would never be the same again. I had no idea as to the timings of the next events, but all I can say is that a fire started to burn and people became hungry for God and His power.

By the time I had left Bible College and married Gillian, friends, family members and Church members alike started to ask for prayer to receive the gift of the Holy Spirit. In all honesty, I had no idea what I was doing, but I did know that God had done something in my life, and I had to share it.

On one occasion, my sister Stephanie arrived at our house, asking for the power of the Holy Spirit. She stood in the middle of our lounge and closed her eyes. As I lifted my hand and started to pray, 'In the name if Jes—' *THUD!* I opened my eyes to find that she had fallen flat on the floor under the power of God.

Word spread like wildfire, and soon after each service people would ask the same question: 'Will you pray for me to receive God's power?'

Sure enough, one by one, the same occurrences happened each time: *THUD!*

One night, after the Sunday service at Church, we were sitting in our little two-bedroomed terraced house, when a loud knock came at the door. Gillian went to answer the door and came back with two people; one that I recognised and one that I didn't. The young lady that I knew from our Church was standing in front of me, with her non-Christian boyfriend in tow. 'I've come to receive the power of the Holy Spirit,' she said.

I looked up at her non-Christian friend and then back at her and said, 'Well, why don't we pray for you later on in the week?'

She said, 'No, I want it now.'

'It's not really appropriate now,' I replied as I glanced across at her non-Christian boyfriend, but she insisted, so I invited them in. I tried to make it clear to her as we sat down on our couch that it wasn't really the right time to pray for her to be filled with the Holy Spirit while he was watching on. I didn't think the prayer would work, and I didn't think it was appropriate. But the more I tried to put her off until the next day, when she would be alone, the more she insisted that she wasn't leaving until I'd prayed for her. I simply said, 'OK then, stand to your feet.'

With her boyfriend perched on the edge of his seat, I manoeuvred her into the middle of our lounge, and placed my hands upon her head. 'In the name of Jesus, I pray…' By the time I had got to that point in the prayer, *thud*. The same thing happened again. She had fallen flat on the floor, seeming totally unconscious and oblivious to what was going on around her.

I looked at her boyfriend, he looked at me. We said nothing. As Gillian and I bent down to make sure she was OK and to continue to pray over her, in what seemed like an embarrassingly silent situation, we were aware that she was not moving whatsoever. Her eyes were closed, and her body appeared to be stiff. A nervous tension began to fill the air in our little back-lounge.

On the outside, I tried to look calm and unruffled, but inside I was panicking. Thoughts ranging from, *Quick, call an ambulance*, to, *I wonder if she died as she hit the floor*, as I couldn't even see one twitch in her body.

Suddenly, her boyfriend spoke up and said, 'Is this normal?'

The only words that came out of my mouth were, 'Yes, of course!'

After what seemed like an eternity, but was probably around four or five minutes, her eyes started to flicker and open, her head started to turn. But then came the words, 'I can't move my body.' As she said those words, fear gripped me.

The young man sitting on the edge of our sofa, breathing heavily into the eerie atmosphere again asked the question, 'Is this normal?'

I said to him, 'Yes mate, it happens all the time.' I didn't want him to know that I had never seen this kind of thing happen before, ever.

In order to bring a little light relief to him, me and Gillian, I suddenly blurted out, 'Why don't we have a cup of tea?'

To which Gillian replied, 'Yes, I'll put the kettle on.'

As we rose to our feet, everything went back to normal, apart from the fact that the girl was still paralysed on the floor. We tried to ignore her for a length of time, while the tea was made, but once it arrived we became more and more aware that she hadn't moved her body.

Deep inside of me, beyond the smiles that I was smiling back at him, I was privately praying, 'Lord Jesus, please, let her not be paralysed, please let her get up.'

After what seemed like an eternity, she then started to wriggle her hands and feet, and all of a sudden life flooded back into her body, and she rose as if from the dead, gave him a hug, me a hug, Gillian a hug and I breathed a sigh of relief as we drank our tea. That girl had been a nominal Christian up until that point, even daring to date a non-Christian young man, which she knew we were against, but after that night, she was never the same again.

A few weeks later, she dumped him and began to move on in her newly revived life; zeal for God just fell upon her. The most amazing part of this, when you think about it, was the fact that none of the people mentioned in these stories had ever been exposed to these kinds of things before. Therefore, nobody from the outside could point a finger and say, 'It's all auto-suggestion,' or, 'Mind over matter.'

Even if some were thinking, *Are these people pushed over or do they fall under the power of God?* it could be answered by the fact that nobody was ever touched. Only the prayer, 'In Jesus' name...' was half-blurted out before they suddenly hit the floor.

This was not a spiritual circus act, but a most sincere move of God upon a forgotten little Church a few years from closure. But not anymore; God had great plans for its future.

CHAPTER 7

Just Married

Two are better than one...

Ecclesiastes 4 v 9

On Sunday 14th of July, 1984, I married my sweetheart bride at 11 a.m.; a day I will never forget, followed by a honeymoon that I have tried to many times!

The wedding took place at the Church that Gillian, along with her mom and dad, had always attended for the past twenty-one years. Strange as it may seem, and against all sound advice that no one gave us, we were about to be married and were still attending separate Churches. It was a practice that created lots of tension that we had not bargained for.

The reception was held at 'The Regis Hall & Restaurant', just a mile away from the Church, in the tiny little town of Old Hill. A cheap and cheerful, council-run facility that sufficed in 1984 for the budget that Gillian's parents carefully scraped together. Thankfully on that day, we meant every word of our vows to each other, as the words 'for better or worse' would certainly be teased over and over again in those early years.

Following the buffet reception, we set off for our honeymoon, in my humble white brown-roofed Austin Allegro car, with the words 'JESUS CARES' emblazoned right across the rear. With our whole lives ahead of us, we set off through the cheering crowd of family and friends not realising that we would be back home much sooner than we anticipated.

Here we were, driving down the country lanes to Shrewsbury, with tin cans rattling behind through every twist and turn as we made our way to Llangollen and our very first four-star hotel experience together. Happiness, excitement, tinged with sadness at leaving everyone behind, became the stark reality at the first leg of the journey. I didn't really bargain for the fact that Gillian would want to phone her mom the minute we arrived at the posh hotel, but I understood. It was her first time in twenty-one years of being separated from the safety and security of a loving family home. What I couldn't understand though, was that Gillian insisted in watching TV – 'Dynasty', to be precise – on our wedding night. Oh well, you can't win them all! I just thought to myself, *This is not supposed to happen,* but it did. Gillian almost seemed oblivious to the fact that I had waited twenty-three years of my life; and it wasn't to watch Dynasty. Enough said.

Because of lack of funds, I had only managed to secure two nights at the Bryn Hotel, so the rest of our honeymoon was to be spent in a beautifully refurbished cottage in Portmadoc for £45. Excitedly, on the third day we drove to our second destination, carefully following every twist and turn, every detailed instruction to our first time alone in a little love nest. Well, whatever kind of nest this was, it wasn't very well put together.

On top of a hill, and like something out of Coronation Street, we both knew as we parked outside our beautiful cottage, which happened to be a dingy terraced house on the edge of a very steep incline, that this was not going to be fun. In fact, it was my first nightmare as head of the house. We smiled at each other as we put the key in the door, hardly saying a word, but knowing that each other's thoughts were going something like, *This better be better inside than out.* But it wasn't; in fact it was slightly worse. Badly artexed walls and ceilings framed a poorly refurbished property that gave us the creeps. I felt despair for my bride, as I knew she liked nice things, and I was responsible, on day three of our marriage, for giving her something quite the opposite. We decided to be positive, in the hope that we would settle in after a few moments. Earlier, we had taken the luxury of going to M&S to buy ingredients for our very first meal together. All I remember was that we had two chicken breasts, which we put in the oven upon arrival.

The kitchen was downstairs in a kind of basement area, and, as I opened the back door to let some fresh air in, I was shocked to find that it opened onto the side of what I would call a cliff. It probably was only a big hill, but it was certainly a steep and dangerous drop. After the chicken had been thrust into the oven, we went upstairs to unpack but, no sooner had we unzipped the cases, than we looked at each other with a look what said it all – 'There is no way we are staying here.' Hastily re-packing, we clambered downstairs. By this time, the aroma of the chicken had started to penetrate through the eerie sense of something that didn't feel quite right.

What was I to do? The chicken breasts must be rescued – even if only half cooked; they were from M&S and were our very first shopping item. There was no way we were going to stay, even for M&S chicken! I hastily took the half-raw offering out of the oven, wrapped it in foil, stuck it in a food bag, then we literally ran out of the house, slammed the door shut, and retreated to the safety of our Austin Allegro.

Over the years, I have tried to imagine what the neighbours must have thought about the honeymoon couple that came and went, never to return. The mind boggles and it doesn't really bare thinking about. We got into the car, and without saying another word, I just drove, until suddenly, the thought hit me, *We're on our honeymoon and have nowhere to stay.* I decided to find a call box and call my dad. As he spoke, the tears just rolled down my cheeks as I had to admit myself and my dad that my best laid plans had come to nothing. I could hardly speak for being choked up, but I managed to convey to him that we had no place to stay and no money to find anywhere. It was only Monday. I embarrassingly accepted the offer of his kindness and his credit card, and decided to drive in the direction from which we had come only a few hours earlier.

Feeling somewhat safer the closer we got to home, we stopped at every Bed & Breakfast that took our fancy, but everyone was full. Now we really did feel like Mary and Joseph but the 'No Room at the Inn' just didn't make it feel like Jesus was with us. Eventually, after having driven for what seemed like three or four hours, I pleaded with a very nice gentleman, the owner of a B&B, that we were at the end of our tether. As I explained our unbelievable situation, he seemed to warm to us, and he found us his best room, which was sheer luxury to our erstwhile Coronation Street cottage on the hill. The only problem I now faced was that I was staying on my dad's credit card, which would have been OK apart from the fact that I knew that they could barely afford this luxury themselves.

We decided that two nights was our limit and when Wednesday came, we were heading back home in the hope that no-one would spot us arriving back at our little two-bedroom terraced house that night, having only left on Saturday. The thought of being asked why we were home was horrible, knowing that everyone's honeymoon is expected to be a fantastic, brilliant, amazing experience, when in reality ours was a total disaster. Well, almost.

We loved being back in the safety and security of our little terraced home, especially as it was filled with lots of unopened wedding presents. Our arrival back was a hundred times better than the honeymoon. We excitedly started to arrange our presents, and make the inevitable call to tell our parents we were home. Once we told people the truth, they started to feel sorry for us, when in fact we loved being back, living in our first little house for the first time. People were so kind to us, which in a way backfired on us, as one lovely Christian couple, who were the parents of one of Gillian's close friends, came around and announced that we could have the use of their caravan during the following week. We looked at each other and thought, Great, let's do it. We both had the fortnight booked off work anyway, so we were free to go to Towyn.

Towyn is one of those places that you should never go to more than once in a lifetime. Our 'once' was about to be had, as we excitedly packed our cases and took to the road for our second honeymoon in the space of just two weeks! There's nothing at Towyn, but we weren't told that. The directions took us to a field, quite literally, a huge field, right at the foot of a Welsh mountain. And there it was as we looked up... a caravan, no bigger than my car. A two-berth caravan right in the middle of a field, on its own, with only one cow to keep us company, along with a thousand flies.

The weather was scorching and the caravan acted like an oven. The nights were totally dark and somewhat eerie, as we sat perched in the middle of nowhere. Flies buzzed, the cow mooed, and Gillian complained. We decided we didn't do honeymoons, and so, yet again, after a couple of days, we said goodbye to Towyn forever and headed back home. Our honeymoon season was now officially over and married life was about to begin.

CHAPTER 8

God Never Forgets

Before I formed you in the womb I knew you, before you were born I set you apart.

Jeremiah 1 v 5

Five weeks after we married, on July 14th 1984, with no job and no idea of what the future held, Dudley Council Catering Department called me to say that they had heard I was back. My two-year break from catering was about to end. I was invited to an interview for the position of Catering Supervisor, and promptly got the job. The job turned out to be one of those that no one wanted; they just didn't mention that the time. Anyway, I didn't care, it was money that I needed; albeit £76 per week and that was for heading up twenty staff and overseeing the whole Meals on Wheels operation, consisting of cooking up to 4,000 meals per week. Only twice, as far as I can remember, did I question God's wisdom in allowing me to do such a job when I had sacrificed my life savings and two years of my life for College. Both those times were in the massive cold room situated just off the kitchen. My question each time was simple: 'What on earth am I doing here?' Both times the answer was the same: 'It's all good preparation.' Well, it shut me up anyway!

Back at the Baptist Church, which by the way Gillian wasn't attending with me (stubborn woman), signs of life continued to emerge following the miracle. I found myself praying, which I had done since I was around fifteen, but on a more regular and structured basis. I began to keep a prayer folder, so that I could pray intelligently, if you know what I mean, and record any results of my prayer. My regular prayer was that God would send us a Pastor by Christmas 1988.

I had completely forgotten about my encounter with God a few years earlier. Either that, or I had chosen not to believe it, as it seemed unlikely to ever come to pass. All I did know was that this growing little Church needed a leader after a break of more than fifty years without one. Weeks turned to months, which turned to four years' worth of prayer for our new Pastor. If my specific prayer was going to be answered by Christmas '88, then God was going to have to work fast, because it was now December of that very year.

The AGM, which was part of the colourful history of the Baptist Church, was about to be endured. So heated were these meetings, that my nan, now well into her seventies, refused to go for fear of her blood pressure getting too high! I fully understood where she was coming from, as on a couple of occasions, I had witnessed arguments that led to people, including leaders, storming out, not to return to the evening's proceedings. I never did find out where they disappeared to on those nights, but one things is for sure though, they must have been cold and wet when they got home, as they always seemed to leave without their coats. On this, the last decision-making event of 1988, the meeting seemed to run fairly smoothly with items such as where the joint Christmas service was to be held, through to who was going to get the 'Tandy's Gifts' this year (a voucher that could be spent in most well-known stores given to the elderly and needy each Christmas). Any other business brought the usual silence, which normally preluded the sighs of thankfulness that we had all made it safely through another evening's proceedings.

On this night, however, something happened that should not have happened. A voice was raised to get the attention of the chairman, Uncle Stanley. The usual silence was broken, as well as an over 150-year-old record of non-interruptions at this stage in the game.

A young woman, about nineteen years old, had dared to speak. With seemingly all the courage she could muster, she bellowed out, 'I would like to say that this Church needs a Pastor, and we all know who it is.'

The silence just got more silent. *Go on then, who is it?* seemed to be the question in everybody's mind, hoping that it wasn't some weirdo that everybody would have to vote on.

'It's... It's... Mark, Mark Burchell.' And with that, she took her seat.

No one knew what to do as this was not on the agenda; well, that is, humanly speaking, but it was definitely on God's. I sat there, stunned. My name was being linked to the role of the future full-time Pastor.

Hang on a bit, I thought, as my mind raced back and forth over the last few years. '*A little child shall lead them... one day you will Pastor that Church...*

send a Pastor by Christmas '88.'

This was it, God had just fulfilled a prophecy over my life from eight years earlier. Had I actually been praying for myself for four years without knowing it? The answer was yes. I was the answer to my own prayer, and the answer to the leaderless Church that had just been saved from closing. Uncle Stanley and the minute secretary remained seated behind the long table at the front of the school room, as it was called then – stunned into silence.

Another voice spoke up. 'I agree,' it blurted out, prompting Uncle Stanley to rise to his feet.

My heart was pounding as the attention was now focused on me. 'Well, erm, that is something that we'd have to pray about,' the standard answer, 'for some time.'

Then almost in unison, several of the twenty-five people in the room all responded, 'We don't need to pray about it; she's right. It's time, and it's Mark.'

'Well, erm, well, we don't have the money to pay a Pastor, so we can't make a decision now.'

Within what seemed a few short, sharp seconds, the whole thing had cold water thrown on it. That was, until my dad suggested that we should seek God and reconvene the meeting for January, when a secret ballot would be taken to decide once and for all, and at the same time ask the people whether they could give more in the offerings. *Great,* I thought. *No one has asked me if I want to go through this, now I'm going to spend Christmas waiting to find out who is going to vote me in and who will secretly have me disqualified for the job I didn't even ask for.* One thing was certain, that little Baptist Church had just voted on something more than the purchase of a new notice board, and everyone seemed to be up for it as they chatted after the service. The only thing I could think was, *WOW! God is faithful. He never forgets.*

It had been almost eight years since He had spoken to me of that very event in that very room.

Over the next few days, just before Christmas, one and another came up to me privately to say that they felt it was absolutely right, and that they would be voting for me. I simply said 'thank you' to each of them.

The big night soon came around. Instead of the usual eerie silence and the same old agenda, there was just one task in hand – the vote. Each person who was a member of the Church, whether present or not, had been given a voting slip. Those unable to attend sent their vote in a sealed envelope via someone else, and those present placed their votes in something that resembled a biscuit tin. I was in the meeting, but obviously not in a position to vote. It was mine to sweat it out, and await my fate. The count was done behind closed doors, in the 'inner sanctum'; the vestry which was just off the little back room where we met. My dad, a deacon, took responsibility for making sure it was done right and proper. After about twenty minutes, the twenty or so papers were counted and registered. Uncle Stanley made it his responsibility to announce the 'winner' of the Pastor contest. 'I am very pleased to announce,' he said, with a couple of nervous coughs, 'that the vote has been unanimous in favour of Mark becoming the full-time Pastor of this Church.'

A round of applause broke out and I breathed a sigh of relief. Not because I felt I'd got the 'job', but because people had actually felt that they could trust me to do it. Following a lot of unusual happy chatter, the meeting was brought to order and a date of Easter 1989 was set for my induction. However, for that to happen, it was explained that the weekly offering needed to increase from £180 per week to £250 per week, and that this would be a sign that we should go ahead. I had just three months to quit my job and launch into the unknown. I still can't remember if anyone asked me if I wanted to do it. I think that everybody just knew that this was it, not least of all me. I was ready for the challenge, but little did I know that I had never known what the challenge was. However, I was about to find out – big time.

The following three months sped by, just as if I was waiting to get married again. Invitations printed, programs drawn up, hymns chosen, guest lists put together, not to mention the announcement to Dudley Metropolitan Borough Council that I was giving up my career for good, to became what was to them, a vicar, of all things.

By the time the big day arrived, the Church had received its reward of faith, as its offerings were now at the agreed £250 per week. From this, all the bills had to be paid as well as the salary for the new Pastor-to-be. The excitement in the Church was tangible. Everyone seemed to be rising to this grand occasion that many never thought they would ever witness again. Early on the Easter Saturday afternoon, all those who were taking part in the ceremony met for a quick rehearsal-cum-prayer meeting. This was followed by a quick change of clothes at home and then back to the Church for the induction ceremony.

A good hour before the start, the place was buzzing, which was something that we were unused to. Gillian was heavily pregnant with our second child, and sported a frizzy perm and a polka dot dress that my dad had bought her (we couldn't afford a new one ourselves). I wore my navy blue suit and coordinated (to Gillian's dress that is) a blue and white spotted tie. As we sat down in the seats that had been especially reserved for us, my heart started to pound, as I began to consider the task ahead. I hadn't really thought of the implications up until this point. All I knew was that by the Grace of God, it would work out, and if not, I could always go back to catering.

Sweet Turf had always been known for its singing, but on this occasion the Church was unusually packed with Christians from all the Churches in the town and beyond. As the first hymn struck up, the volume was incredible as people genuinely worshipped God that night. I had decided to start as I meant to go on. Nervously I had installed a 'Mickey Mouse' set of drums, which were placed on the right side of the Church, at the front, and on the opposite side of the pipe organ. Guitars, let alone drums, had, up until this point, been viewed as instruments of the devil and were a definite no-no. Crafty, I had them installed the day before my induction, so that none of the old leaders would know they were there. In fact, the first time they would be seen was when they walked into the service that night; by then it would be too late to do anything about it. As the chorus section of the service was introduced, I took a deep breath as I knew the bet would be starting for the first time since 1810. Fortunately the singing was so loud and enjoyable that the drums just became part of the majestic worship that night – something I will never forget. By the way, the drums stayed, even though, I was shortly to find out, the moaners didn't.

My dad was the first to give a heartfelt speech on

behalf of the Church and in my support, as he would – he was my dad after all. I was then called upon to give my 'inaugural' speech. Nervously, I addressed the crowd and began to tell them about the secrets that they obviously knew nothing about. I unfolded the events of the last eight years of my life, and concluded with the words, 'I have no choice in this at all. God has called me, therefore I must obey.' A round of applause followed, with a brief challenging message by the late Sydney Price, who laid his hands on Gillian and myself and inducted us into the ministry. Esther, our first child, clung to Gillian's legs and wandered round and round in circles, much to our embarrassment.

What an amazing turn of events, I thought to myself. *Who would have thought it?* God had called the shyest, most unqualified person to lead the Church. With the average age of the congregation close to sixty and mine at twenty-seven I realised the significance of God's word over my life: 'A little child shall lead them.'

Well, I have to say that just like my wedding day and honeymoon period, there soon came the reality of the marriage. And so it was with the reality of pastoring the Church. Doing something that had never been done before became increasingly a challenging experience for me, to put it mildly. There seemed only one way to tackle it, and that was to learn from experience, albeit mainly bad ones in those early days.

The Church was run by a group of men that I had inherited. They felt it was their job to lead me rather than the other way around. Frustrated by the lack of progress I could make with such men, two of whom I had addressed as Uncle since I was a kid, I began to pray to pray for a way forward without them. Uncle

Stanley and Uncle Horace had to go. The only person I needed to stay was my greatest supporter at fifty-seven – my dad. I didn't have a plan really, but just decided to try a couple of things to see how they went. The first thing I decided to try was to seriously ask God to remove Uncle Stanley by taking him home – to heaven that is. I had concluded that almost at eighty, he had done his best and was now ready for promotion. No sooner had I sent in my request than God sent back a reply – 'Sorted.' After a life of health and happiness, Uncle Stanley peacefully went to be with the Lord six months later.

WOW, I thought, *this is easy. Who shall I try it on next?* It was obvious, Uncle Horace was to be next on my hit-list. But as I got to prayer, this still small voice of the Holy Spirit told me in no uncertain terms that Uncle Stanley's promotion was a one off, and that I would never develop my leadership skills by praying people out!

'No, Mark,' the voice of the Holy Spirit said, 'you will have to deal with this one yourself.'

Great, I thought. *I'm not looking forward to this one bit.*

Uncle Horace was a cougher. He would cough loudly every time I said something that he disagreed with, and, into the bargain, he and his wife would haul me over the coals every time I visited them. It was usually to do with the modern NIV translation of the Bible that I had introduced. One notable occasion was a passage from scripture in which the NIV had translated 'vessels' as 'bowls'. This was too much and was something that she did not feel was at all fitting in the Bible!

So, I prepared myself for the uphill battle of removing Uncle Horace from the position of life Deacon. It was going to be a very steep hill if he was still alive; and he was, just about.

I tried every which way at the monthly Leaders' meetings to get him to retire but he wouldn't budge. I offered him a gold watch, stereo system, recognition and suchlike but he was having none of it. He became more and more of a trial to me and the advancement of the Church.

Until one day, I received a letter from him stating that, following my persistence, he had resigned and would stand down immediately. I have to say, I felt sad for him, but I knew in my heart of hearts that it had to happen or we could never move on. Following the removal of my two elderly adopted uncles, I began to build a younger team around me from the steadily growing church, until I had a group of what I felt was tried and trusted men numbering five in total. *At last,* I thought, *we can move on*, and in the intervening years the Church began to fill and grow in numbers. Within the space of five years, it was ten times numerically larger than when I started. *If this continues,* I thought in my naivety mixed with faith, *we shall be a few thousand soon.*

Little did I know then that we needed more glorious subtractions, before we would be even a few hundred.

CHAPTER 9

One Foot in the Grave

Where there is no vison, the people perish.
Proverbs 29 v 18

History has it that the little graveyard, which, in 1971, had been tarmacked over at the front of the Church, had been full for over 100 years, since the plague of Netherton – nasty. I was about to find out how true that was, as I began to make plans to build an extension on the front of the old Church. It would incorporate much needed offices, inside toilets and a foyer.

As the JCB rattled on site in December 1991, we had already been granted the authority to dig up the graveyard, as no claim could be made against us if the last burial had taken place more than 100 years ago. Tombstones galore started coming to the surface, not to mention other things, suffice to say that half of the extension was built over a burial site, including my new office – spooky.

Twelve months earlier, it had become apparent, to me anyway, that we needed to provide some much needed up-to-date facilities to bring us into the 21st century. Toilets were still the originals, hence they were outside; cold, dark and smelly. The entrance porch to the old church was called the vestibule, whatever that meant. It was just big enough to house a few people side-ways on, as long as they kept in single file. My makeshift office was situated in the back kitchen at this point, and was also used as the vestry. The one-bar electric fire did little to inspire me, let alone keep the damp away on those cold, sermon preparation mornings. All in all, it was time to take the plunge, and build something that would solve all these problems.

Plans were drawn up and two estimates were invited from two separate companies. The first, was for nothing more than a plastered square box on the front of the Church with no expensive extras, and came in at a grand total of £35,000. The second was for a much grander design, incorporating oak doors, special lightning, indoor planters, a Parana pine ceiling and beautiful hand-finished brickwork. The cost was a staggering £75,000 and threw us into a panic as to which one we should choose.

Based on two trains of thought that we had, the first being that you get what you pay for, and the second that we should do things with excellence as it is God's house, led us to the conclusion that the more expensive building was the one that we should reach for. *Brilliant,* I thought with excitement. *Let's do it!* I made a plan to speak with the Church members, and to put to them our financial forecast for how we could achieve it. In my naivety, I thought that everyone would be up for it. Little did I think that the only one who wasn't, was the only leader who dealt with money every day – in a bank. *Drat!* I thought. But no, we should go with the majority and go for it – and so we did.

The financial plan was to get as many people as

possible in the Church, to pledge as much as possible over a three-year period. Everyone was then to write it down on a piece of paper, and hand it in on the proposed Gift Day Sunday later that month. I was informed by the sceptics, that the last time this was done was for new carpet and only £800 was raised. However, faith just kept rising within me, and when the Gift Day arrived, I was nervously optimistic that we would achieve something a little more inspiring.

That Sunday, as the pledges were counted in the Vestry, I stood at the front of the Church, whilst the congregation chatted as they waited for the results. The paper with the sum won was quietly slipped into my hand and when I opened it I couldn't quite believe as my eyes as I said the figure: £37,000! Almost half the total sum had been pledged in one go. WOW – what a fantastic encouragement. The people of the Church were elated to say the least. And so, in December 1991, the grand project got under way. Mud, gravestones, and odd bones flying here, there and everywhere, made way for the new facilities, as years of history was dug up.

I had never done anything like this before, so I hadn't got a clue about how the whole thing would work. What I hadn't fathomed out was that the £37,500 in pledges was not real money, or at least most of it wasn't anyway. A good portion of it was three years away now the building had started. It was only when the first bill came in for the first stage payment that suddenly realised how naïve I had been. We hadn't got a mortgage in place, and we hadn't got any of the pledge money in either, and now I needed £26,000 by the end of the month. 'HELP!' I cried. I had clearly not thought this through at all, and was really doing it in faith, believing that

God would meet our needs – how silly.

I quickly started to panic as the numbers flashed before my eyes, along with the embarrassment of having to tell them that we couldn't even pay for the first bill. If only I had listened to my leader with the common sense gleaned from working in the bank. *I know what I'll do,* and quickly ran across the street to the Church's local bank and asked to see the manager there, telling him it was very urgent. Unfortunately, he didn't share the same faith as I did, and told me, in no uncertain terms, that he could not lend us money there and then. I walked out with my head down, feeling so deflated, and so stupid. *What a mess,* I thought. *I've only been Pastor for less than two years, and I'm already leading the Church into financial ruin.* From that day to this, I still don't know what happened; apart from the fact that the first bill was miraculously paid, and we did secure a mortgage from the Baptist Union, and we did get an interest-free loan, and we did finish the building on time! And into the bargain, the prayer that we had all prayed that the ten-year mortgage would be paid off in five, became a reality, as in year six the building was debt free.

The night before the grand opening, I called all the core people together and walked them through into the beautiful new extension. Tears ran down my face as well as the faces of many others, as we contemplated the good of God in giving to us such a lovely new and necessary facility.

The opening celebration on the following day saw the Church packed, as everybody rejoiced with us at what had been achieved – well most, anyway. God had bailed me out... or had he?? I think He just did what He does best – He responds to simple child-like faith; a lesson that later was to stand me in good stead. It would be that same faith that I would need to look to, the same God, but next time for hundreds of thousands, and then further down the road, several million!

CHAPTER 10

The Tent

Therefore I tell you, whatever you ask for in prayer, believe that you have received it and it will be yours.

Mark 11 v 24

My old school playing field was to be home to the thousand-seater tent crusade, planned for the summer of 1992. A well-known healing and gospel evangelist was booked, along with the massive tent, toilets, generators, banners, posters and security caravan. The 'TENT' was used as an acronym for 'The Event of Ninety Two.' Little did I realise that there was to be an event before the event that came totally unexpected.

It was a fine summer evening, when, in preparation for the crusade, the Church met for prayer on the Crusade site, long before the tent arrived. As the people made their way back up the grassy bank of the Hillcrest School and playing fields, I was lingering behind, contemplating the task in hand; that of organising the Crusade, and raising £7,000 to pay for it. As the summer sun sank low in the sky, suddenly, I was overwhelmed by the sound of a voice, an almost audible voice, but one that was inside of me; in fact, it was the same voice that years earlier had spoken to me about pastoring the Church. I knew it to be the voice of God. As I turned and looked around, shocked at what I'd heard, I saw, as though for the first time in my life, the large, empty parcel of land running alongside the Crusade field. It was as if the finger of God had pointed exactly at where He wanted me to look, as the voice boomed within, 'BUY ME THAT LAND.' Instantly, I knew that I had just had my second encounter as a Christian with the voice of God, and I had to respond. What should I say? What could I say? What I did say was, 'Well, if this is you, God, you'll have to confirm it by telling someone else. This is too big for me.'

God heard my plea, and within weeks, I had started to record happenings relating directly to the sale of the piece of 'Holy Ground'. One man drove past the side and came to tell me that he'd seen a new church building being built on there, and needed to tell me. That he did, but I never showed any emotion, or gave anything away that I'd been told by God to buy it.

Page after page rolled in over six months, so much so that I knew beyond a shadow of a doubt that God had confirmed His word and that I should act.

I decided that my first move was to tell one of my closest leaders at the time, and so I asked him to meet me on the site. The following Christmas, I decided to tell the congregation to come to Church in their wellingtons on that first Sunday in January, as we were going for a mystery walk. The walk from the old Chapel to the new site was less than ten minutes. Once there, I read from the pages of my notebook that old story of God's voice and all of the confirmations. I'm not sure how many people fully grasped the significance of that winter's morning with a difference, but I know that for me, it was full steam ahead to get things moving. I hadn't got a clue where to start, so I did a little investigating and found that the land was indeed for sale. Two brothers owned it, as well as the garage just fifty yards from the site. With the other leader, we made an appointment to see the one brother, and left suitably deflated as he seemed almost dismissive of our interest, knowing that we were from the Church, which probably meant to him – no money!

As time passed, the asking price was revealed to us as £200,000 for the whole site, which included a warehouse as part of the land. The numbers seemed far too high for me to contemplate or even believe for, so I decided to try something and see what would happen. *If this is God*, I thought, *I'll offer £100,000 and they'll accept it and somehow I'll have the money.* But they didn't and I didn't. Getting straight to the point, they flatly refused the offer out of hand, and so God didn't have to supply it. *Phew! That was close,* I thought. *What if they'd have said 'yes'? Then I'd have had to tell them I was bluffing.*

The only way to tackle this, I felt, was in prayer. I gathered a few believers together, and told them that we would be trespassing on the land every second Friday at 7 a.m. before anyone could spot us. We should be praying for God to do a miracle and send us the money to buy the land that He wanted. Spring and summer turned to winter as we met that year, but still no miracle. The seasons came and went almost four times before a glimmer of anything, when right out of the blue, we received a call from the company selling the land, saying that they wanted to sell to us, so I re-submitted my original £100,000 offer. Once again, they flatly turned it down. No one could have known during those four years that God was preparing a young business man to fund salvation in our Church that year.

A lovely young lady and her young children had been invited to our Mother's Day service that year, and at the end of the service, she gave her life to the Lord and was transformed. Into the third week of her attendance at Church, I ended my message by stating that God didn't just want road sweepers in His Church, but he also wanted brain surgeons and company directors too. Little did I know that her husband was a company director, and was sitting just a few yards away in his 7 Series BMW in the car park, waiting for his wife to leave Church, as apparently he did each week. As soon as he was outside, she told her husband that the Pastor had said that he wanted him in Church next week. I suppose I did, in a roundabout way. The following Sunday, her husband, aged thirty, a successful businessman, decided to give it a try. Within ten minutes of entering the service, he broke down in tears and gave his life to the Lord.

Several weeks later, I got a call from him asking if we could meet. As we stood in our kitchen, chatting away, he told me that God had spoken to him and because he was selling his business in the next few months, he was going to give a certain amount to the Church in obedience to what God had said.

WOW!

As the weeks rolled by, I desperately wanted to believe this was the answer we'd been looking for, but I decided to put it right to the back of my mind.

The last thing I needed was a massive disappointment when he told me that the deal had fallen through or something like that. Well, true to his word, he called me after several months of negotiations and wrote a cheque following the sale of his company, which turned out to be £126,000. This indeed was God meeting our need for the new Church site. When I called my leaders together that night, they almost fainted and cried at the same time. I had never heard such a shout of praise go up to God from the little Chapel that weekend, as I told the congregation what had happened. Now all we needed to do was purchase the land. Dad and myself made our way to the business offices, ready to do the deal, which had now been set at a lower price of £150,000. But, as their architect tolled out the plans onto the boardroom table for the two-acre site, a very disturbing picture emerged.

The businessmen had realised that they could make a good financial killing here, and had taken it upon themselves, behind our backs, to have their architect design several houses, two warehouses and car parking together with a rather small Church right at the back of the site and out of the way. The spokesman for the group piped up, 'We don't think you'd want all the land to yourself, and we can make a lot more money by building houses, so we've decided to take this route and you get a new Church as well.'

How I stayed seated for so long I don't know, but the Holy Spirit rose up within me and I stood to my feet as bold as a lion. 'Gentlemen,' I said, 'we have come here today, as you know full well, to purchase the whole of this site, and you have deceived us. God has told me to buy this land for Him, so I dare anyone of you to try and lay one brick on it, and I promise you, you will come to nothing. The whole thing will fail the moment you touch this land, it belongs to God.' And on that, we both walked out.

By 9 o'clock the next morning, the meeting had been reconvened, and this time the group of men were much smaller. 'Mr Burchell,' the owner said, 'we have considered what you said to us yesterday and we were up until very late last night thinking things over.' *I bet you were*, I thought. 'Before we talk business, why don't you talk to us about the Church?' So I did. For twenty minutes solid, and gave them everything. No sooner had ended my little speech, than the spokesman said, 'Well, we have decided to let you have what you wanted. The whole two-acre site is yours for the £150,000. But can I ask first of all, how will you pay for such a site, Mr Burchell?'

'Cash,' I tried to say as humbly as possible, but in reality I think it was I the tone of my voice that sounded like, 'You didn't expect me to say that, did you?' The look on their faces was wonderful. In March 1998, we effectively became the new owners of 'God's two-acre Miracle Site.'

Hmm, I wonder what's next. I thought, as Dad and I went back to tell everybody the good news that we were now the owners of the land.

CHAPTER 11

Where There's a Will,

There's a Way

Like a partridge that hatches eggs it did not lay is the man who gains riches by unjust means, when his life is half gone, they desert him, and in the end he will prove to be a fool.

Jeremiah 17 v 11

I will never forget the look on my wife's face that day, as I stood at the doorway to our gutted bathroom, hands covered in tile adhesive. For weeks, I'd spent every spare moment ripping out and renovating the family bathroom, and on this particular afternoon, I was halfway through the laborious job of tiling from floor to ceiling. At this stage, our home office was situated just across the landing, so I could see Gillian busily working away at the computer as I tried my best to do a professional job as inexperienced tiler.

As I glanced up, Gillian's head was peering round the office door with a look of absolute amazement, along with the words, 'You'd better come out and have a look at this.'

'Can't it wait?' I asked, making gestures towards the ceramic glue all over me.

'I don't think you'll want to wait when you read this email,' she replied.

Half-heartedly, I marched across the landing, and looked unenthusiastically over her shoulder to see what all the fuss was about. 'Read this,' she said, pointing to the email on screen.

Impatiently, I started to read, and after the first few lines realised she was right; the more I read, the more I definitely wanted to read more. I was completely flabbergasted to learn that the Church had been left a legacy in a will. The details were forwarded to our Church from a barrister who had been left with the responsibility to discharge the wishes of a missionary couple who had both been tragically killed outright in a car accident.

The story unfolded from the email, that this Christian couple, who had been serving God for many years abroad, had accumulated vast amounts of land and property which had been bequeathed to a Christian charity deemed to be worthy of the money. My mind raced back and forth over the email, looking for signs that this was a sick joke, but all I could see was Bible verses and names of men of God that I had recognised from Christians television.

The barrister, who was writing, had obviously been touched by God, because he spoke of Jesus changing his own life, and he wanted to make sure that the honourable wishes and indeed the legal requirements from the will of the couple were carried out.

As I stood there, with my hands setting in

adhesive, I froze to the spot as I tried to contemplate the size of the numbers mentioned at the close of the letter. Was it £10,000? No, it must be £100,000. No still not enough for the noughts.

'Oh my word,' I said out loud. 'We have been left £1,000,000 in a will!'

'Read it again,' Gillian spouted. 'It's not 1,000,000, look at the noughts. It's one, and seven noughts.'

'No, it can't be,' I said, over and over again. 'It's ten million pounds. No, this cannot be true,' I counselled myself and decided to write it off as a prank and a sick one at that.

I walked back over to the bathroom, and as I reached down into the adhesive bucket spreader, I shouted to Gillian, 'Why would somebody do that to us knowing that we are earnestly praying for a miracle of finance? Surely they wouldn't stoop to such depths.'

(Now you know why one of those walls in our bathroom has wonky tiles!)

As I lay in bed that night, tossing and turning, I allowed the sum of money to take hold of me. The more I thought about the email, its Christian content, Bible verses, and sincere story of a changed life, the more I began to plan what I could do with it. I thought about giving one million here and one million there; what a fantastic blessing, I thought, to help so many other Churches and people. I eventually went to sleep believing that the whole thing was a miracle from God.

The next day, I excitedly arranged to meet with my trusted leaders in order to share the potential good news of our windfall. There was stunned silence that night, as each of the three men listened intently as I read the contents of the email. After a time, we stablished that the best way forward was to check it out and find out where it had come from. The next morning I busily emailed back and forth with several searching questions. One thing led to another, and before long, I was holding conversations with the "brother" by mobile phone, who was a few thousand miles away.

The long and short of it was that the money was being held in a high-security bank in the homeland of the missionaries, and upon us signing the certificate and the security company sending us one back, we would have to pay a security fee in order to have the money released and shipped and released to a holding somewhere in Amsterdam, where we would be shown the money and upon paying the remainder of the security fee, £10,000,000 would be ours. All of you that right now are thinking that this is going to end in tears – read on, and enjoy the rest of the journey.

Several phone calls later, to two different continents and even the police and airport authorities, my brother-in-law Tim and I boarded the 6 a.m. flight from East Midlands Airport to Amsterdam, hanging on tightly to a not too small amount of currency that Tim had stumped up for the rest of the security deposit. Nervously, we walked into the terminal at Schiphol Airport after landing and looked around to find the well-dressed, tall, dark gentleman that had been described to us earlier in our correspondence. True to his word, he was waiting, and yes, he looked the part.

During the flight, we had discussed between us the things we would never do, one of which was that we would definitely not get into the back of a car, feeling it was too risky and highly suspicious under the circumstances.

However, breaking the rule immediately and sitting in the back of a Mercedes five minutes after we landed, seemed the only way to be transported to our pot of gold, even if it was by three large men, one with a six-inch scar down his face.

So off we went and twenty minutes later we were escorted into what looked like a fairly derelict block of offices – gulp. *Not a good sign,* I thought.

Scarface led us through a series of corridors under lock and key until we reached a large, locked, inner office in which four other men sat around a boardroom table. They greeted us with a handshake and then immediately asked us for our passports, and although neither of us felt that this was looking good, and certainly not the thing to do, we realised in the presence of now six large men we couldn't really argue.

After being told where to sit around the table, I noticed to my right a large wooden chest which was padlocked. Opposite, sat the boss and next to him was Tim. I was asked if we had brought the money, and when they had counted it, they signed a form to say we had paid.

The tension we both felt in that room became so tangible that we both began to wonder if we would ever see our wives and kids again. As the meeting progressed, each of the men in the room seemed to grow more agitated and edgy, making us feel trapped and uncomfortable at the same time.

As the 'paperwork' was quickly completed, the boss signalled to one of the other burly guys to unlock the chest and reveal its contents. I will never forget what we saw. Piled to the top, and neatly wrapped in polythene, was what appeared to be tens of thousands of crisp notes, all sealed up inside the chest.

To my surprise, as I glanced back and forth, I noticed that my name was written in red pen in large letters on the polythene – REVEREND MARK BURCHELL.

Quickly, a bundle of notes was pulled out by one of the guys and shown to everyone in the room, and then it happened: the boss made much of the fact the there was a watermark in the middle of every note, rendering every single of them unfit for legal tender.

No sooner had we stumbled on this potential 'spanner in the works', than the man began to put a surgical mask and pulled out, as if from nowhere, a large syringe and started to draw into it a liquid from a sealed container.

Tim's face was a picture. *This is where we die,* he thought, and on that, quickly pushed himself away from the table, stood to his feet and said loudly, with panic in his voice, 'Whoa, what's going on here? What are you doing?'

Good question, I thought, from my seated position across the room, as I glanced back and forth at the bouncers, the one with the six-inch scar on his face, and now one with a mask and a syringe.

Amazingly, I felt quite calm as the guy then explained that the red dye on the notes could only be removed with a special substance, which had amazingly been sent with the money, although only enough for us to do a quick demonstration.

He then proceeded to squirt the substance over the £10 note in a dish, and hey presto, the red dye drifted off it as if by magic.

Then came the bad news; the special potion was only available in Germany and in order for the money to became legal tender hey would have to fly one of their guys over there as quickly as possible. They would have the solution and clean the notes within two days. Following that, the process would be complete and the £10,000,000 would be ours.

We were then told we would leave and travel back to the airport with the well-dressed gentleman who would then prove to us that the £10, freshly freed from its mysterious red mark was in fact legal tender.

To be honest, the thought of us both getting out of that place alive seemed like good news, no matter how bad the news which we had just received. Sure enough, the guy wandered up to the Exchange Bureau in the airport and got the note authorised as the real deal. 'What happens from here?' Tim said, as we realised we had deposited a large sum of money with them and left with nothing, up until now anyway.

'It's simple,' he said. 'We fetch the solution and then we call you in two days when the notes have been cleaned.' And with that, he left us with a handshake.

As we sat there late that afternoon in Schiphol Airport waiting for our flight home, we looked at each other, and slowly but surely, it dawned all over our faces that we had been stitched up good, right and proper. This was one BIG scam.

There was no will.

There was no way.

There was no money.

There was no genuine story.

There was no barrister.

And there was definitely no 'money back' guarantee.

Just a gang of scam artists preying on a vulnerable Church that they had sussed needed several million pounds and decided to give it a shot.

The only consolation was that although they had fleeced us to a degree, they had not managed to do it, as we found later, to the extent they thought they would. Yes, we had been hooked at the first level, but the big money that they had played for was never going to be handed over.

Here's what didn't happen...

As we arrived back at East Midlands Airport that night, my phone immediately rang and the smart guy broke the news. He proceeded to tell me that the solution to clean ten million was now going to cost us £38,000, which when we paid, we would then get the full amount. As I told him, in no uncertain terms, that he had been well and truly sussed, and it was the end of the road for them all, he ended the conversation rather abruptly. Suffice to say, we drove back home in total silence, just glad to be alive, even if there had been a couple of twists – *So much for my gift of discernment,* I thought.

Days later, phone call after phone call followed from scammers, each with a different voice to the previous one, and more threatening in its tone, to hand over the next payment or else...

I eventually silenced them by threatening to arrive back with the British Police in tow. That seemed to do the trick; we never heard from them again.

The following week, things returned back to

normal as I walked into our offices, although I was still feeling somewhat vulnerable.

I have to admit though that I had the last laugh, when two days later the scammers, who seemed to have suffered a brief memory lapse, sent us another email using different names, but promising the same sum of money, using the same concocted story, down to the last letter.

Lesson learnt once and for all, I mused, as I promptly pressed delete on my computer, thinking of the old adage, once bitten twice shy.

CHAPTER 12

Eleven Years of Waiting

We do not want to become lazy, but to imitate those who through faith and patience inherit what has been promised.

Hebrews 6 v 12

After buying the land in 1998 and all the excitement that had brought about, life returned to normality again and the Church ticked along nicely, with fairly healthy growth, some folk leaving, and me wanting to quit a number of times along the way – all fairly normal stuff really. I started to think about what God would want on the land, and came to the conclusion that a new Church fit for the King and fit for the 21st century would be the order of the day. My biggest concern was to find the architect who would hear me out when I said I wanted to build a Church that looked nothing like one.

After all, if people no longer graced the Church door with their presence, then why build one? Most people I found didn't go to Church because they had already been! Apparently once was enough. *Why not build a modern, people-friendly, conference-type building that looked like it belonged in this generation?* I thought. I began to take notice of the newly built Waterfront at the Merry Hill Centre, one of Europe's largest shopping centres, just five minutes from where we lived. As I drove, and sometimes walked around the beautiful new office blocks, hotel and shopping complex, I began to ask myself who would design a place like this, so I decided to find out. After several phone calls, I was given the name of the architects who designed the whole thing, Level Seven Architects was their name, and little did I realise that they were based in offices just five minutes from my own Church office instead of where I thought they would be, in London or some distant place.

I nervously picked up the phone and arranged for them to come and meet me at my little office, situated in the new extension, built over the graveyard. I had no idea what to expect, and when three business man got out of their S-Class Mercedes, I thought I'd bitten off more than I could chew.

'Gentlemen,' I said, as I ushered them into my little space, 'please take a seat,' which was a joke almost, as it was nigh impossible to get more than three people into that little box. 'I have a dream,' I kicked off, 'a dream that wants to see a new Church built in this community, and I want to know if you would be interested in helping me. My only problem is that I don't have any money. If you would like to be a part of this amazing project, then call me. Here's my card.' That was it, apart from a few niceties, then off they went, never to be seen again; or so I thought.

Two days later, Level Seven became our official architects and were destined to be with us for the long eleven-year journey ahead. Initially, they asked me to write down a description of the building that I envisioned, rather than draw what I thought it should be.

I started with:

1. A building to seat 1,000 people.

2. A large foyer that would look and represent something like a hotel.

3. Dedicated rooms for kids.

4. Plenty of space for youth to hang out

   ...and so the list went on.

Level Seven immediately put one of their architects on the job. His name was Reg. It was not until the first boardroom meeting several months later that I found out that 'Reg' was actually named 'Alun'. I felt rather a fool when I discovered that no one else called him Reg – only me.

After the meeting was over, I took him to one side and asked, 'Why did you introduce yourself as Reg when your name's Alun?'

He promptly replied, 'That's my middle name, I just use that with friends.'

I thought that was a compliment.

Several weeks went by, and finally the drawings arrived. And there to top it all, Reg turned up with a beautiful model that he had hand constructed as a scale model of the new Champions Church. *WOW,* I thought. *This is amazing.* I immediately began to dream of the incredible new Church that would one day soon be built.

A design team was brought together and the project was worked on until it was just right. That was, until it was costed out at over £4.5 million, a figure that turned out to be beyond our means, no matter how much we wanted to believe.

We so much wanted it to work that we took on a professional Fund Raiser, all to no avail. We posted out letter and images to seventy businesses and local millionaires, and finally filled out a large lottery fund application, but that too, like everything else, came to nothing. It was to be built from within. People's generous giving, coupled with faith in God was to be the order of the day. We were on our own, if you know what I mean. The words – 'One with God as a majority' came to mind and so we plodded on.

After several more months of work at the drawing board, we took the plans to the local council for planning approval, and without a problem, they passed the first time. However, the only thing that came to anything were the fees that had accumulated over what was something like three years of hard work for all the consultants. As much as I hated to admit defeat, the dream had run away with itself. The costings and the fees had run into tens of thousands, and still no building, just bills to pay.

I was wracked with sadness, disappointment, embarrassment and of course guilt that we had spent money on a project that was not going to happen. I think many of the people working for us, as many as five companies at one time, probably resigned themselves to the fact that this was just too big of a project for a relatively small Church with little money.

Without anyone formally saying so, the project just died in the water, but thankfully it never died in people's hearts, not least of all mine.

A further two years passed by, and, after feeling the strong urge to move forward again, I sought advice from as many people as possible; I even went as far as an award-winning architect in Cape Town when I was there on a speaking engagement.

The long and short of it was, everyone said, 'Simplify it, and phase it. Build now what you need, and build later what you can do without right now.' It seemed like the only logical conclusion and the only way forward for us.

In the absence now of Reg, who in the meantime had left the company, Trevor, the Managing Director, took a hold of the project, and began to get rid of many of the 'unnecessary' cost elements without taking away too much from the actual look of the building.

We decided that we needed a main auditorium right now as that was the only thing we didn't have, or at least one big enough to house the growing congregation. We 'toed and froed' for weeks, with my stubbornness refusing to let go of the original design for some elements of the new building that I had become attached to from the very first design. But, the result was a simplified, more cost-effective building that was split into two or three phases, should we need to, with the first phase being costed at £1.9 million plus fees and extras.

Dudley Planning Committee demanded that we take it back through full planning again, at a cost of £10,000, but we had no option.

In November 2008, the Planning Committee would meet and once again our building would be recommended to the planners for approval. That was, if no one appealed against us with an official complaint. Friday of the previous week was the deadline for anyone to register such a complaint against us, and by Friday lunchtime everything was going just fine. That was until my office phone rang with the news that, at the last minute, a complaint from a local resident, whom we knew, had been officially lodged against us. My heart sank as I wondered how many more hurdles I could leap before tripping and failing to get up again.

The following Monday arrived as leaders and I made our way to the Council Chambers at Dudley Council House. We looked like five men dressed for a wedding as we took our seats and awaited our fate. The planning application was read out and the objector was asked to sit down. We all took a deep breath, prayed like mad and sat there in silence. To our amazement, the person launched an attack on the local Council for not keeping their word in informing the local residents of the change in our plans. But then, amazingly, started to speak in our favour and ended up by giving us glowing report in front of everyone, just as if he had ordered to so by God. One by one the committee spoke in favour of the project and gave us glowing recommendations and then the verdict: Planning Approval granted. YIPPEE! A sigh of relief and an incredible desire to shout out, 'Thank you Jesus,' was muffled by the auspicious occasion and surroundings that we found ourselves in.

At exactly that time, our Monday night service was in full swing, and was earnestly praying for God's favour on us as we met at the Council Chambers. As the planning meeting finished soon than anticipated, we went to the local McDonald's just round the corner for a quick 'cuppa' before descending on the service to break the news.

The roar of praise and relief, mixed with shouting, whistling and clapping almost took the roof off the old 1810 building as the people learnt of the great news. Once again, the green light for go was shining brightly as we contemplated the goodness of God in helping us overcome with faith and patience the last eleven years of waiting.

CHAPTER 13

Stop, in the Name of the Law

When the righteous prosper the city rejoices, when the wicked perish there are shouts of joy.
Proverbs 11 v 10

I was just settling down to my usual morning of study at home when the phone rang that Tuesday. The voice on the other end sounded breathless and panicky as it blurted out, 'They're on the land. The travellers are moving onto the land!' Two weeks earlier, one of the guys in the Church had noticed that the large bolts, on which the main gates of the Church's new two-acre site hung, had been carefully cut through.

I was warned that someone was making preparations to get onto the property, so I told the guys to security wire the gates together, to prevent us from being easy prey.

This particular Tuesday morning was that day. The day to take over Champions Church's new building site, and turn it into a caravan park; one that neither the neighbours nor the town, let alone the Church wanted to happen. It was the office that had called to let me know, and had also started to send staff members quickly across the road just a thousand yards away, to where the site lay. In response to the frantic call I had just received, I jumped into my car and with jeans and leather jacket donned, I sped the one-mile journey to get the scene as soon as possible.

As I arrived at the T-junction opposite the site, which, by the way, was very busy main road, I witnessed a procession of vehicles all lining up in preparation to access their new plot.

Unfortunately, I was too late to stop the inevitable two vehicles, complete with caravans, which had already made their way to the back of the site... with others following.

Without hesitation, I shot across the road, mounted the pavement and cut off the entrance by parking my car smack bang in the middle of it, bringing the flow of cars, wagons, caravans and you name it to an abrupt halt.

I jumped out of my car and knew I was a man on a mission that day. Mayhem erupted as it became clear that my car was staying put. Cursing coming from every direction, with the occasional death threat, which was like a water off a duck's back. The Youth Pastor and Worship Pastor, along with a couple of female office staff, appeared quickly on the scene alongside various neighbours and other anxious people.

Miraculously, we had thwarted the takeover plan by-and-large, and now all that remained was for someone to encourage the people and vehicles who had already gained entrance to leave the site.

That person, I knew, was me. I marched up the first acre, and boldly strutted my stuff up the second, as I came face to face with the leader of the pack.

'You're leaving,' I declared.

After a few expletives, the guy told me in no uncertain terms that I couldn't do a thing about it and he was going nowhere.

'Watch me,' I said. 'This land belongs to God and so I happen to believe you are religious too. So if I were you, I wouldn't trespass on God's property.'

'So you're a Christian, are you?' he said. 'Well if you are, then you'd let us stay.'

'No way,' I said. 'This land doesn't belong to me; it's God's, and He ain't giving permission right now for anyone to stay on here, so turn around and go and join your friends. If you don't, I'll have two hundred people surrounding you by tonight.'

'Are you threatening me?'

'Yes,' I said.

'So what will they do; fight us?' he enquired.

'No,' I said. 'They'll be here to pray, so I'd move now if I were you.'

As I turned and looked back at the entrance, I was aware of a crowd that was gathering, and watching my every move. In the distance, the police, who had been called, were gathering in a group around the entrance trying to calm things down. I thought that I ought to have a word with them, so I made my way slowly back down the field. 'Good morning, gentlemen,' I said, as the officers approached me.

'Would you like us to come and force them off

the property, and if necessary, arrest them for trespassing, sir?' the sergeant said.

'Yes please,' I said, quite shocked that they had asked me for permission.

'We've brought the dog van as well,' he continued. 'Do you want the dogs?'

'Yes please,' I replied.

'How many?' he queried.

'How many are there?' I enquired.

'Four.'

'Right-ho, sir,' he said, and went back to the dog van.

With a new-found confidence, I made my way back up the site, knowing that sooner or later, police, dogs, and two of my guys would also be along.

'You're going now,' I boldly declared to the leader of the group, who was already making our field his home with a few other relatives.

'Get in your van, or I'll push them off you by hand,' I said.

After several exchanges of conversations, expletives and unpleasantries, the police intervened, and the guy got into his van. With not so much as a fight, he signalled to his mate to drive the vehicles off.

The last memory I have is of several people pushing the last caravan through the gates; it had been less than an hour from start to finish.

People cheered as the whole convoy moved on, out of the town, on their way to the next 'spied-out' plot.

'Well done, sir,' the senior policeman said, as he and his officers gathered around me. 'That is the quickest removal of travellers that has ever happened in the history of our force. Usually, it's six months, court cases, and tens of thousands of pounds; it unbelievable we got sewn up in less than an hour. There is just one question though.'

'What's that?' I said.

'The guys are asking, "Who are you?"'

'I'm the Pastor of the Church that owns this land,' I replied.

'Do you know,' he said, 'we thought you must have been the Police Chief that had been called in when we saw you directing everything.'

I laughed.

'No really,' he said. 'That's why I asked you about the dogs. I was taking orders from you or so I thought.'

I just thought to myself, this was a modern-day miracle in which we had just been involved, and didn't even realise it at the time. God had somehow given me a uniform just the right fit for that day to carry out His purpose. What an amazing God!

As the traffic cleared, the police dispersed, and the neighbours went back into their homes, I sensed that everyone had witnessed a battle that was not of this earth, but had been directed from Heaven itself. Everyone was left open mouthed as they went back to their normal lives.

CHAPTER 14

Give and You Will Receive

Give and it will be given to you, a good measure, pressed down and running over.

Matthew 6 v 38

We were no strangers to giving money to other Churches and people. Upon receipt of the large cheque that we had ever received, from which we bought the land in 1998, we immediately designated £12,500 to give away. £2,500 went to pay for publicity that had been ordered by a great evangelist friend of ours. As he sat in my office one day, he shared his need with me about his outstanding bill at the printers, God simply said, 'Pay for it.' So we did.

Several nights later, I had a vivid dream in which I was standing at the front of a particular Church that I knew, as the dream played out, I handed them a £10,000 cheque for their building fund. In the dream, I was actually speaking there the night that I gave that cheque. When I awoke, I casually thought about it and said to God, 'If you want me to do that, You will have to get me booked to go to that Church.'

Three days later, I received a call from that same Church, asking me to go and speak there one Sunday night. As I sat in the Pastor's office, he wept, as I handed over the £10,000 cheque. He confided in me that in thirty years of ministry, no one had ever given him anything.

Now it was 2004, and for some reason, late one night, as I was getting ready to go to bed, I felt strangely compelled to check the Pastors' conference that I'd heard about and which happened every year in Phoenix, Arizona. The Pastor was the very well respected and well-loved Tommy Barnett. For almost thirty years he had faithfully encouraged Pastors from all over the world at his renowned Pastors' School, which attracted 7,000 Pastors every year.

That night, I told Gillian my feelings, and decided to stay up and research exact dates and how much flights would cost. Knowing that Phoenix was right near the west coast of America, with a flight time of around eleven hours, I immediately knew that it would be beyond my realm financially. As I typed in the exact dates for a direct flight with British Airways, I couldn't believe my eyes, so I checked again. It stated £97 each way. 'That can't be right,' I thought, as I went through the whole exercise again, but sure enough, it was right.

I went to bed that night knowing Arizona – here I come. Why, I didn't know.

The next day, I decided to call my brother-in-law, Tim, and asked if he would like to join me. Without hesitation he said yes, and three weeks later we were on our way. We didn't know why, just that there was a reason why God wanted me there.

We were picked up from the airport by a couple of folks from the Church, who immediately made us feel at home. We had arrived less than three hours before the first night of the conference started, so with no time to waste we drove straight to Phoenix Firs Assembly Church; a Church of around 14,000 people, with a 7,000-seater auditorium. Without so much as a wash or a meal, we were ushered into this incredible auditorium and seated just to the left, with 6,998 other Pastors. The service went on and on, as we battled with the heat and jet-lag, with both of us on more than one occasion finding our mouths wide open as we fell asleep, with Tim letting out the occasional snore.

By the end of the night I couldn't help wondering, why on earth had we come all this way? What good is it going to do us? Little did I know that the answer would come the very next day.

I'd heard Pastor Tommy Barnett before, and really warmed to him as a person and as a Pastor. Added to the fact that we'd had a good night's sleep now, Phoenix seemed to be a good place to be that day, as we were seated listening to the great man himself.

The Church had three massive balconies. And on that morning we'd been seated in the second one, right up in the gods, peering down at the stage. For some unknown reason, I turned to Tim and said, 'This morning, I know that I'm going to be standing right down there at the front of the stage.' He just smiled back at me as the service continued.

Pastor Tommy then asked a guy to tell the most incredible story about how God had blessed his business over the last ten years as he obeyed God, giving money away. We were blown away by his incredible yet humble story. As soon as he'd finished, Pastor Tommy got up and said: 'This is our special offering day for the Dream Centre in Los Angeles.

Every dollar that you give today is going towards the facility that will help drug addicts, prostitutes, the homeless and the hungry in LA. Right now, I'm going to ask you to give your very best seed to help renovate the Dream centre (an old hospital).

The moment he said that I knew that this was why God had wanted me there.

It was now late February, and by this stage, as a Church back at home, I had a set a target for our building fund to reach £25,000 by Christmas that year. I knew that this was a 'big ask' and in need of God's miraculous touch to get anywhere near it. We had, however, got a good start as we had already managed to raise, by people's generous giving that is, around £120,000.

In the second balcony right then, my heart began to pound, and then it happened – the figure of $40,000 came to my mind.

'You are to give $40,000.'

I knew that whether it was my own thoughts or God's voice speaking, that that number was the right figure.

I quickly started to do the old calculation thing in my mind took over. The sums went something like this: 'That's £22,000 which leaves us with less than £100,000 in our building fund, and we need £250,000 by Christmas.'

Somehow the numbers didn't stack up naturally speaking, but I just knew that this was one of the biggest tests I'd ever had from God. I turned to Tim before I could talk myself out of it, and told him the figure.

He just smiled and said, 'Well, you'd better do it then.'

I had no time to talk to my leaders, no time to do any 'red tape' stuff; just plain old 'do it now' stuff.

No sooner had I got the figure fixed, Pastor Tommy said, 'Those of you right now with a special offering, I want you to come right now down to the front of the stage. I want to meet you here and shake your hand.'

By the time I'd made my way down to the front, I found myself waiting at the end of a queue of people just wanting to be a part of the answer for the Dream Centre in Los Angeles.

Minutes later, the tears flowed down my face as I presented the pledge on behalf our Church for $40,000 to Tommy's son, Matthew, Pastor of the Dream Centre.

I just felt an incredible high as those few seconds unfolded, and equally so as Matthew turned to his father, pledge in hand and said, 'Dad, this man had come all the way from the United Kingdom, and has brought this great offering.'

After a few more tears and exchanged words, Pastor Tommy started to pray over me.

'Dear God,' he said, 'you know how I've always longed to build a great Church over in England, and now I'm too old to do so; I ask you therefore to do it through this man. In Jesus' name, Amen.'

On that, I shook his hand and walked away, totally engulfed by the presence of God, with the full knowledge of why we had flown 6,000 miles – to give and to receive.

I didn't know it then, but since that moment at the front of Phoenix First Assembly Church, I have bumped into Pastor Tommy and Matthew Barnett more times than I can recall and ended up taking teams of young men to the Dream Centre to serve and see first-hand what we had sown into on that day.

So, what did happen with the building fund, you may as well ask. Well yes, it did go down to £98,000 in March of that year, but then supernaturally it started to rise again.

One guy in our Church alone was able to sell stuff on eBay with a promise to God to give the Church all of the profits. In December that year, he brought a cheque for £10,000 from his part-time trading. With just a few days before Christmas remaining, we decided to bring the target to a close at one of the December service. People were asked to bring in the best offering and when the total was added up, we were just £300 short of a quarter of a million pounds. Glory to God.

The place erupted, and one lady stepped forward and gave the shortfall, taking us to our target of £250,000.

Would we have achieved it had we not been obedient? Make up your own mind – Matthew 6 v 38: "Give and it will be given to you, a good measure, pressed down and running over."

CHAPTER 15

In for a Penny, in for a Pound

According to your faith
Will it be done to you.
Matthew 9 v 29

Until now every bill relating to the new Church had been met in full. It just seemed that, whenever we started to move forward, God supernaturally started to send increased income to meet the need. Architects' fees, ground preparation costs and planning fees had now been added up to a massive £350,000 including the purchasing of the land, and still no building in sight.

The mine shafts alone, that had been located on the two-acre site, cost £32,000 to be filled and capped. As much as the figure scared me from time to time, I just knew that without spending this kind of money, we would not be able to start building anyway. God's hand was upon me to believe for miraculous finance; even business leaders now wanted to meet with me, as they too recognised something supernatural happening in this money thing.

What started out many years earlier in believing

God for a few pounds, had now grown to trusting Him for a few million. I believed that God could do it completely by Himself, but I also felt for us to become serious players in what had become a big venture, we needed to have more than just faith when it came to explaining where we were going to get the money from. I quickly learnt that faith is the language of the Christian and the language of God, but it doesn't carry much weight when you're trying to convince a contractor that God will supply our need somehow, sometime, somewhere; especially when that need is over two million pounds.

In order to make us a match for the job in hand, I began to make enquiries as to which banks would be interested in loaning big money to a small Church. Surprisingly, I found it quite easy to get bank managers that specialised in commercial loans to come out and meet me for a chat over coffee. Three of the major high street banks sent their leaders to meet me in my office, each suggesting that I should put a business plan in place and get the level of cash to a much more realistic level. The problem was faced was that although the cash for the building fund was coming in, it was just as quickly going out, as we were faced weekly with invoices for yet more work that had to be done relating to the new site.

The banks recommended that we needed a least half a million pounds in cash to get anywhere near being taken seriously for the rest of the loan. After working for days flat out and putting together a viable business plan, one by one the banks each walked out on us, each stating the same thing – 'We love what you are doing. We believe in your vision, but it is too high a risk for us to take it on. Goodbye.'

Disappointed and disillusioned with the whole thing, it was back to the drawing board, or so to be more truthful, back to prayer.

For some time now, Kingdom Bank had started to feature on the radar screen of many Churches, but it had never felt like a serious contender to loan us any money, albeit being a Christian-run bank. The bank had recently become a more serious player in the big boys as it started to grow and attract more customers, especially from the Christian scene. This was due in part, I think, to the fact that they gave away 10% of their profits to needy causes, something that people have always felt attracted to, including ourselves.

Feeling like there was nothing to lose, I called the manager and found out that they were in favour of lending money to Churches in order to let them expand and grow. A meeting was arranged at their head office, and together with two trustees we travelled the two-hour journey for our first chat. That afternoon, as we drove back to Dudley, we felt good about the day, and even felt that the bank liked us. Our parting felt positive, as they said that they would come over to us next time to see what we were doing.

We seemed to click the second time around also, as we took them out to our beloved Starbucks for a coffee and lunch with the Chairman of the bank. It seemed like an eternity from that day, waiting for them to decide whether our figures stacked up from the three previous years' accounts. One day, I waited nervously for the promised phone call from the manager, which revealed both good and bad news.

The good news came first – they were willing to loan us finance on the basis that our books looked good and that they believed in the project.

'What's the bad news then?' I nervously asked, waiting once again to have that terrible sinking feeling that I had experienced regularly over the last months.

'The problem is...' came the cautious reply, 'because we are a relatively young bank, we do not have the lending power of most other banks. In fact, the level of lending is set by an independent body that oversees the bank. Unfortunately, we can only lend a maximum of £675,000, and that's it.'

Sure enough, that sinking feeling came, as by now I was sitting with my head in my hands.

'Well, thank you so,' I said politely, 'but, to be honest, it's neither here nor there. It's a lot of money to some, but when you need 1.25 million it may as well be nothing.' And with that, our call ended with rather shallow and disheartened goodbye.

'God,' I said, 'if you want this building, then You will have to help me here. Everything is just a resounding "No", and I need a "Yes" right now.'

The Church got to hear of the current problem, and so once again, we made it a matter of joint prayer. If were to get this project off the ground, then we needed God to intervene.

One afternoon, I unexpectedly got a call from the Kingdom Bank manager.

'Hi Mark,' he said, 'you know how I said that our limit was fixed? Well, today the governing body of the band has been to give us our twelve-monthly check-up, and have raised the limit of our borrowing power.'

'Yes, go on,' I replied, detecting a more positive note in his voice.

'The bank's board have also met with me today, to review your case following the meeting, and for the first time in the bank's history, we have decided to loan you the maximum amount possible.'

By this time, I was thinking, *Just spit it out!*

'The amount that we are able to loan you is £1.2 million and that is what we have agreed is available to you.'

I was absolutely ecstatic. For the first in two years of knocking on every door possible, here was the answer to our need. A Christian bank loaning to a Christian Church the maximum amount in their history – WOW! I could only thank them and thank God at the same time.

Within a couple of weeks the proposals were sent through, and for the first time, in around fifteen years, we had the official pieces of paper that made us serious players in the world's eyes.

As far as I was concerned, God could and would still miraculously send us money if He so wished, without any loan whatsoever, but this was important in as much as we needed those pieces of paper to prove to man, who only deals on that level, that we could now make serious headway on starting the new Church project.

CHAPTER 16

God, I don't need a miracle tomorrow...

With God, all things are possible.
Mark 11 v 24

It felt like it would never happen, but seventeen years after my encounter with God to 'Buy me that land,' the ground-breaking ceremony finally arrived – it was now March 2009.

It felt quite surreal as I crouched on the snowy site in my fur-lined overcoat with Peter MacPhillips, one of the directors of the construction company, as we posed for the cameras that day. In my early thirties, I'd always dreamed of this day, and now in my late forties, it just felt like another day. Although I'd never physically seen the start of the project with my human eyes, my eyes of vision and faith had lived out the scene a thousand times before.

A week later, the contractors, mobile offices and machinery rolled onto the site with great interest from the community that had secretly been waiting for the building to start as much as the Church folk.

One slight technical problem was lurking in the background, just enough to take the edge off the excitement of seeing a JCB rolling off the back of a low-loader and onto the site. The problem was that although planning permission had been granted back in November 2008, it had been passed subject to certain conditions being met in the process. All the conditions were attached to what was known in the highways jargon as a section 106. This was an agreement between the contractors, the Church and the Council, regarding the new road system that had to be created at the entrance to the new Church.

The conditions were so onerous, that solicitors had already been going back and forth and still had not reached an agreement that was suitably met. The long and short of it meant that for the Church to be given the green light for the project to officially start, it would do so at 'great risk' as planning permission could not be signed off without the agreement being reached on the 106.

Blow it, I thought to myself. *I've waited seventeen years, knowing that the last time we moved house as a family, I instructed all the windows to be replaced at 'great risk' before we ever signed the contract* (something I don't ever recommend, but in this case there was no-one living in the run-down property). *It all worked out OK then, so let's give it a go with this,* I thought.

'If God's on our side, it'll be OK – it's just a technicality,' I counselled myself and my trustees. And so we pressed the button for all systems go.

In my mind, I thought that everything would be signed off by the Council and the solicitors within a week or two, in which case only the foundations would be under construction and officially we were

OK until the building rose above ground level for all to see. This, I knew, would take at least six weeks to happen.

Five months later, it felt like we must be the only Church in history that dared to build without officially having possession of the aforementioned planning permission and 106 agreement.

March tuned to July as spring turned to summer and the building got higher and higher; so much so that there was no mistaking that we had made a start. In fact, we were more than halfway through the project and everyone's head turned as they passed by. It got riskier by the day, knowing full well that if Dudley Council wanted to, they could technically halt everything and even make us take it down.

No matter how much I tried to force myself to face reality and press the 'stop' button, somehow, I just had an incredible peace that all was well – or so I thought.

So far we had managed to stay debt free for the five months into the build, having paid over £400,000 from our cash reserves that the people of Champions had sacrificially given over the years. (At this point, a quick calculation revealed that over £8,000,000 had been given and poured into the project over the years.)

The crunch came in August, when I knew that our £1.2 million mortgage with Kingdom Bank would need to kick in. This wouldn't have been a problem apart from one not-so-small detail: the dreaded planning permission. Without it, the mortgage could not be released, and without the mortgage, we were faced with an incredibly embarrassing situation – the next stage payment for £186,000 could not be met.

With only £40,000 left in the Building Fund, there was no way we could move forward. We were well and truly up to our necks in it, and, bar a miracle, there was no way out; we were doomed.

I decided to email the Project Supervisor that day, along with our solicitors, the bank and a number of other key people. I simply outlined the fact that we had just ten days, or less to get the mortgage authorised, which meant we had around five days to get planning permission and the 106 agreement signed off, which after five long months seemed impossible.

As I checked my emails the next morning, for any glimmer of hope, I was totally knocked for six as I read the Project Supervisor's reply. He basically told me, in no uncertain terms, that should the payment be late, the contractor had warned that he would have no choice but to get his men to walk off the job, leaving us liable for all costs incurred. My mind raced back and forth as I contemplated half a building standing in a field for my kids to finish years later.

'What a fool you have been,' a voice whispered deep into my soul. 'You should have never started; now who's going to take the rap for this? It's all your fault. You should have waited,' the voice said.

The trustees were informed of the dire situation as we met that night.

'All we can do is pray,' I said, as we sat around our dining room table. Looking back now, the meeting was incredibly light and easy, and we spent as much time laughing together as we did in serious conversation. We just knew that but for God, we could do no more.

With just eight days now to go before the project

folded, I rose as usual to pray the very next morning. My prayer was simple, as I held my head in my hands once more. 'God,' I said, 'I don't need a miracle tomorrow... I need one today!'

It was an earnest, heartfelt, honest, direct and loud cry from my heart. We needed an immediate miracle or I feared that God's name, above everything else, would be brought into disrepute.

That day, if I'd never seen before, I saw God's miracle timing come into its own. It was masterpiece of perfection, in response to faith. After five months of waiting, the planning permission and 106 agreement were suddenly signed off and sent to our solicitors. In turn, our solicitors informed the bank's solicitors, who then received the go-ahead from the bank to release the money earlier the following week.

Phew! I thought. *That was close,* which was the understatement of the year, but I knew that it was God's eleventh-hour plan, experienced only by those who persist in faith.

With just three days to go, the contractors received the £186,000 into their account and few were any wiser that it had been down to the wire.

I breathed a sigh of relief when the Director of the contractors emailed me later that next week saying, 'Thanks for sorting out the money so promptly, Mark, much appreciated.'

I couldn't help myself as I sent my two-worded reply: 'No problem,' as I pondered yet another modern-day miracle. With God there is never a problem, always an answer. He'd pulled it off again, as only He could.

CHAPTER 17

Faith is for Beginners

If you have faith as small as a grain of mustard seed, you can say to this mountain, 'Move from here to there,' and it will move. Nothing will be impossible for you.

Matthew 17 v 20-21

I discovered early on in my Christian life that you don't need great faith to do great things; just a little faith in a great God is all it takes. I also discovered that faith operated like a muscle, in that you had to begin with small exercises in order for it to grow and become stronger.

One of my earliest recollections of exercising my simple faith in God was for the grand total of £5 so that I could buy something special for my girlfriend! Now it's a million times that figure for our current and future needs (for the building that is – not my girlfriend – I married her 25 years ago). The key I found was to see that faith was for beginners. By that I mean you have to start somewhere; if you don't start, it will never happen for you.

Here's a story that will help you to make a small step of faith. It's just the start of a daily adventure with the Living God.

It was Wednesday night, and I was booked to speak at a small but lively Church in the south of England. The rule is that I never travel alone, and on this occasion, I'd ask four guys from the Church to come along for the ride, knowing that it was going to be a fairly tedious four to five hours round trip, not including the service.

On the day that I was due to go, I distinctly heard that still small voice within, the voice I had recognised over many years to be the voice of the Holy Spirit. 'Whatever they give you as a gift tonight, you will not take one penny of it for yourself, but will immediately post it on to that couple that you know, who are personally in need,' He said.

I had met this couple several years earlier, when they had been pastoring a Church further down the south coast. I'd recently spoken to them on the phone, and they had reluctantly revealed to me that they had not been paid by their Church for several months due to the fact that the Church was in a very difficult financial position. It was this couple that God spoke to me about, saying that I was to send them the money.

To be honest, I didn't really think about it too much, as I knew it wouldn't be a great sacrifice to give away what I had anticipated would be petrol expenses for the trip or maybe a maximum of £50.

I'd been told by the Pastor of the Church that we were only to expect around thirty-five people at the service, and what was if the wind was blowing in the right direction. He was true to his word, because when we arrived, there were thirty people plus the five of us – spot on.

Halfway through the service, I started to get really

uncomfortable, as the Pastor suddenly took to the platform and began to lay into the people about how they should honour the visiting speaker and give the very best offering they had ever given. Of course, the source of my discomfort was the fact that he was giving an incredible heart-felt speech, while all of the time unknown to him, I was about to give it all away. And even more so because, unbeknown to my wife, any money that I received and which we could well do with, was not coming into our house that night. In fact, I knew I would be well and truly out-of-pocket.

People reached into their bags, pockets, purses, wallets and pulled out cheque books as the offering baskets were passed around. As they did so, all I could think was that these poor folks were giving for the first time to somebody they had never met before, who was about to give it to another couple they'd never met before and didn't know that it was going to happen.

What shall I do for integrity's sake? I thought to myself, in those split seconds.

'Let's welcome our special guest speaker for tonight, Pastor Mark Burchell,' said the Pastor, as people rose to their feet to welcome me with a cheer.

'Please be seated,' I said. 'First, I need you to know that I am under strict instructions from God to give away everything that you have just give me in the offering. Therefore, I want you to know that if you feel that is not what you want to happen with your money, then please come and take it back out of the basket...'

Not a soul moved, and no one did take any money back, and at the end of what turned out to be a great night, I was handed an envelope containing a cheque for the amount given.

Then, just as I was leaving for home, the Pastor took me to one side and said, 'There is a second cheque in this other envelope, and I am under strict instructions that this is personally for you. The couple that have given it have insisted that it must not be given away.'

'Okay,' I replied, with a kind of embarrassed look going on between us.

Finally, the five of us got into the car and chatted late into the night as we made our way back down the M5.

As I dropped them off one by one, I began to think about how I was going to break the news to Gillian the next morning, when I told her that I had given our much-needed money away – again!

The house was all in darkness as I walked through the door at something past midnight. Wearied by the journey, I threw the two envelopes onto the kitchen worktop and contemplated what would be inside each of them as I put the kettle on.

I decided not to wait until the morning to open the envelope containing the money that I was to send to the needy couple in a few hours' time. Past experience of speaking in different places in the UK told me that this would be at best, just enough to cover expenses or at the worst, a tenner.

I contemplated, as I had done earlier, that it wouldn't be a problem to give it away, but wondered why God would want me to give such an insignificant amount to a needy family.

Oh well, here goes, I thought, as I ripped open the envelope and pulled out the cheque. I couldn't believe my eyes when I read the sum that was far greater than I had ever been given before – £350!

It suddenly dawned on me there and then that I'd committed myself to over God whatever, and I was about to give away the biggest speaking gift that I'd ever had, and into the bargain, I would be breaking the news to Gillian of our blessing that had now been promised to someone else. As I stood there in the kitchen thinking selfishly of what I could have done with this much needed money, I just went into a speech to God that went something like this:

'God, you've told me to give it away, and that's what I'm going to do. But how are You going to beat that? I know there's a cheque in the other envelope, but even if it's for £50, then all it's done is cover my fuel, and You know that we are trying to finish the decorating and can't afford to so. I know that whatever I sow, that's what I'll reap, but I just don't know how You're going to beat £350. You know I went there tonight to bless and encourage a few people, and I didn't go for the money. But Lord, as You can see, these people have given amazingly and now it's on its way to some other family...' and on and on I went with my little speech trying to get my point across.

'I may was well open the other envelope, for what it's worth, before I try to get some sleep,' I said to myself, hearing a rare cynical tone to my own voice that night.

I tore open the second envelope that I knew was definitely earmarked just for me, and as I pulled out the cheque, I almost fell to the floor. It read £2,000. Two... thousand... pounds.

I held my head in my hands in shame that night, as I realised that I had doubted Almighty God's wisdom in questioning what He was doing.

The old words, passed down to me flooded my mind. 'God's no man's debtor.'

I slept like a baby, and early the next morning awoke to the sound of Gillian's voice asking if I'd had a good time the night before.

'I didn't even hear you come to bed,' she said, through a big yawn.

'Yes, great thanks,' I replied. 'By the way, I received the biggest gift that I've ever had.'

'Wow,' she said. 'That's good; we can finish the decorating.'

Then I blurted out, 'The only problem is, I've already given it away, so don't get too excited.'

The look on her face said it all. 'Oh Mark, why do you always give money away the moment you get it, when you know we need it ourselves?'

'I had no choice. God spoke to me and told me to give it to that couple we know who haven't been paid for several months.'

With a long pause, Gillian looked up and said, 'OK, I can't argue with that then.'

'No,' I responded, 'but the good news is that I was given a second cheque, that I was told must not be given away.'

'Who by?'

'I don't know. I was told it was a couple in the service, and guess how much for?'

'I've no idea,' she said. 'But I guess it can't be as much as the one you've given away.'

'Well, you're wrong. It's for £2,000.'

Absolute silence – a second miracle in a 24-hour period – enough said!

Someone once said, 'The way you serve tennis will determine what sort of ball comes back at you.'

The Bible has always said, 'Do not be deceived, God cannot be mocked. A man reaps what he sows.'

Today, why not step out of the boat yourself...? I know you'll risk sinking, but the greatest thrill is that you'll also risk walking on water.

CHAPTER 18

The Last Lap

**Let us run with perseverance
The race marked out for us.
Hebrews 12 v 1**

I don't cry easily; I suppose like most men I just bottle it up, and deal with it internally. However, there is only so much a man can take and as December 1st kicked in, the floodgates just opened that afternoon.

With the grand opening just over a month away, and the building looking far from complete, I trudged my way back through the mud to my car that was parked on the make-shift construction site car park. I had just finished my weekly site visit.

The massive container that was shipping in the 828 cinema-style seats had been stuck in customs, and, as if to add insult to injury, the three specialist seating guys who had been flown from China to fit the seats were refused entry into the building, due to health and safety rulings that stated that they had to go through a site induction. Sounds easy enough – that is, unless you can only speak Cantonese.

I found the three guys sitting in the back of a hire

car that afternoon, just after being told the news that unless we found an interpreter, they would not be fitting any such seats; a matter made much more serious because their return flight was in less than ten days' time.

Into the bargain, I had just had words about the mud on the newly laid carpets, and now to top it all, I was trying to carry two large boxes of newly designed carrier bags for the bookshop, which had been wrongly delivered to the site office and now been thrust into my hands.

As I tried to wrestle with them through the mud, whilst at the same time reaching to find my car key, I heard my phone ring for what seemed like the hundredth time that day. Just as I reached for it, I saw the box of new bags split open and about to land in a pool of mud at any second.

'Are you OK?' said a familiar voice on the other end of the phone.

And that was it. I just sobbed and sobbed right there in the middle of the car park. I couldn't take any more. The 'Palace of Praise' had become too much for me.

I immediately felt better after a good cry – that was, until half an hour later, when I received an incredibly well-timed and encouraging text from one of our young people. I cried again, in fact, it happened three times that day!

The Church service on the previous Monday night, back at the old building, was packed as usual as I outlined our need to pray for an interpreter for the very next day, otherwise the workers would be sitting it out yet again.

Thankfully, at this point, the prayers of previous day had been answered, and the seating container was on-site. Now we needed another miracle – an immediately available, Cantonese-speaking Englishman or woman, on the cheap, in the middle of Netherton and out of work! It was more difficult than finding a needle in a haystack.

So pray we did, and by 3.30 p.m. the very next day, Garrie, a fifty-three-year-old Cantonese gentleman, rolled up to the site. Where he came from and how he got there is still not clear, but apparently, a series of chance meetings and phone calls led him to find out about our need and immediately respond.

Whatever you choose to believe about that one – I know what I believe.

Within hours of Garrie's arrival on the scene, the Chinese workers were mobilised and raring to go; so much so that they finished all 828 chairs a whole day before they were due to fly back home – phew!

The chairs looked fantastic; the building was coming together at last.

I have to confess that I had never felt pressure like this is all of my forty-eight years. It has undoubtedly been the greatest challenge in my whole life. For the last two months, I have woken up every night in fear, only to fall back to sleep hours later in faith.

The reality of living life on the edge, and not knowing whether, on any given day, you are going to fall off, has been tempered by my total trust in God for over thirty years now. In which time, if I have learnt anything, it is that faith is spelt R-I-S-K.

Every day, I have to answer to myself just one question: do I listen to fear and stop in my tracks, or do I keep moving in faith knowing that God will supply our needs in order to see the building complete?

With just twenty-two days to go before completion, and seven weeks before the grand opening, I have made my decision yet again; feel the fear and do it anyway.

The stark reality, though, is this: if God doesn't do something fairly soon, we are sunk.

What no-one knew, that is apart from my closest leaders, was that the spiralling cost of such a building, plus all the extras that we wanted along the way, left us with a massive £500,000 shortfall with less than a month to go.

Our special Gift Day, which had been announced earlier in the year, had gone ahead in November. The goal of which was £150,000 in order to pay for the seating and part of the sound system. Once again, the Church had risen to the challenge, and counting up the cash, cheques, pledges, loans, not to mention a gold set of teeth, rings, necklaces, an old log book for a motor home and even a Roland piano, brought the final total to £165,000.

I calculated that the people of Champions Church had given something just short of *one million pounds* towards building the new Champions Church over the last few years. These people are truly amazing.

I knew that, sooner or later, I would have to face up to the biggest test of faith I had ever gone through; that of addressing the shortfall with the contractor.

The money was due to run out just before our last-but-one stage payment, but, with a further payment in December plus all the extras, it meant that we well and truly needed God to pull off an incredible financial miracle yet again.

I arranged to meet the contractor for casual lunch on site, knowing that I was going to have to tell him about the situation. No one else could or should have to do it. The buck stopped with me.

On the Monday night before my meeting, December 7th of 2009 to be precise, we held our last ever main service in the old Church building, which had seen 200 years of history pass by.

That night, the Church was extra packed, even squeezing right into the foyer, with no room to breathe. Emotions ran high and tears flowed as we looked back over the decades that had shaped many lives inside that building, and then we quickly changed directions as we looked forward with anticipation and excitement to the Grand Opening of the new Champions Church in January 2010.

Right at the end of the service, I asked people on this occasion to bring an extra special offering to the front of the Church, and place it in one of the offering bucket.

It was to be our last offering in the old Baptist Chapel.

As the people queued to bring their feelings that night, what I didn't know until afterwards was that some people had run out of the service to the cash point over the road in order to give their best, whilst others wrote pledges on scrappy bits of paper. And to top it all, one lady on the service felt challenged to go home and invest her life savings into the project. That night, the reality was that all gave some, and some gave all.

On this final occasion, everyone sensed that there was a miracle taking place in the house, as the presence of God swept one more time in the 200 years of history. Later that night, I received a phone call to say that, yet again, the people had given incredibly with a total amount of £42,000. I was blown away with people's generous and sacrificial giving.

As I sat over lunch the very next day, in one of the portacabins on site, the contractor thankfully beat me to the big question that had been lying heavy on my mind, as he enquired as to how things were going financially at the Church due to the recession.

I was able to answer him with a massive positive, as I shared with him about the latest two Gift Days, one of which had only happened a few hours earlier. I knew that in that moment, it was crunch time. I told him that we were now running out of money, and were waiting on the next £500,000 to come in very soon; meaning that his request for £525,000, which I knew was coming later that week, was not going to be met. Every penny we had right now was just over 300k, leaving us, on that invoice alone, with a deficit of 225k.

His response was music to my ears, as he simply said, 'Not to worry, Mark. Pay me what you can now, and we'll roll the shortfall over the next month.'

I leaned back in my chair, took another bite of my roast pork baguette and breathed a sigh of relief. His final comment before we took a quick tour of the building was simply, 'We know that you're not going anywhere, so don't worry.'

I have often found that God doesn't always supply vast amounts of money for the miracle, but He always turns up and makes a way. In this instance, God simply made a way.

That Tuesday, I trudged through the mud back

to my car in peace, rather than in pieces, knowing that once again God had got it all sorted.

The new Champions Church was almost complete, and looked amazing. The seventeen-year journey has been worth every pain, and I wouldn't have changed it for the world.

Right now, an almost complete state of the art facility stands tall, as a testament to God's faithfulness and to His Glory, on what was a disused and ugly piece of land.

From the beautiful 'hotel-like' foyer, right down to the toilets, every detail shouts out a message of excellence – after all, it is God's house and He deserves the very best.

The 'Palace of Praise' – phase one, has almost come to its completion and is ready for thousands of people of every age, every race and every colour from every nation to come through its doors for the first time and experience the life-changing power of Jesus Christ, to whom I owe my life.

As I write, I don't have the much needed half a million pounds, but I do know that it's on its way, right now.

As I often say, I don't know what the future holds but know who holds the future.

In fact, the next time you see me, stop and ask, and I'll tell you how it all worked out.

Myself, 18 months and my brother, John, aged 4.

The original Sweet Turf Baptist Chapel - 1970s.

The old chapel when we started to see a revival of people coming to Church.

The room where I attended Sunday School.

On the way to our honeymoon.

The new extension to the Chapel Completed.

The tent Crusade.

Me Baptising my Sister Stephanie in 1987.

Newspapers headlines the day after Planning Permission was granted.

Gillian, my wife of 30 years and our dog, Harvey.

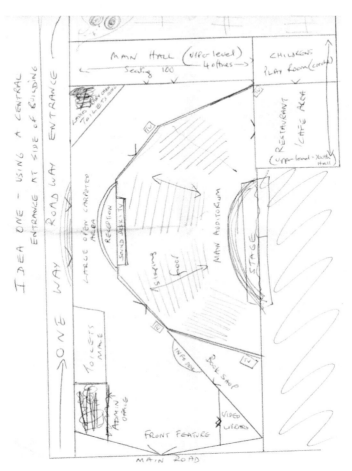

The original Sketch I presented to Level7 in 1998.

The original sale board advertising the two acre site.

The Deacons and Members of

Sweet Turf Baptist Church, St. Giles Street, Netherton

invite you to

The Induction and Ordination of

Mr. MARK BURCHELL

into full-time ministry

on Saturday 25th March 1989 at 7p.m.

The invitation sent out for when I became the Pastor.

ABOUT THE AUTHOR

Mark has been married to Gillian for 35 years.

They have three children and two grandchildren, and live in Dudley, West Midlands.

At the age of 27 Mark's life took a radical turn, from French chef to church pastor.

This is the candid and humorous account of how he took a tiny ailing village congregation into the internationally recognised place of worship that it is today.